D1131331

ANIMAL ATLAS OF THE WORLD

182 Original Paintings by
Melvin R. Bolden
Ann Brewster
Jo-Anne Coons
Alex Gnidziejko
Franklyn Hansen
Richard Harker
Danforth Robinson
William Welsh

Illustrations checked for accuracy by Sydney Anderson, Ph.D.,
Associate Curator, American Museum of Natural History.

ANIMAL ATLAS OF THE WORLD

E. L. Jordan, Ph.D.

HAMMOND INCORPORATED
MAPLEWOOD, NEW JERSEY

Contents

C · 1

Foreword and Acknowledgments

In the title of this book the word "animal" has been employed in the sense of "mammal." It was felt that "mammal atlas" would have been too awkward a word combination for a heading, and "animal atlas" was chosen as a substitute.

The form of an atlas for a book on the mammals of the world is different but in accord with our generation. Interest in wildlife is stronger and wider than ever before, and as a result of today's mass communications knowledge of our globe, even of its remote corners, is broad and general. The present work with its animal portraits, descriptive text and range maps, together with its survey of the most famous nature preserves on five continents, combines the attributes of wildlife and geography in a novel fashion.

The data used in this book (approximate weights, measurements, ranges, etc.) have been checked with the most authoritative work in the field, *Mammals of the World,* by Ernest P. Walker, Florence Warnick, Kenneth I. Lange, Howard E. Uible, Sybil E. Hamlet, Mary A. Davis, Patricia F. Wright; published in three volumes by John Hopkins Press, Baltimore, Maryland, 1964. This monumental work of 2,269 pages is based on 50,000 monographs, articles and other items representing source materials from all over the world, and I am most grateful to its authors and publishers for their permission to let me check my data with their findings.

The information of the world's wildlife preserves and animal sanctuaries was graciously supplied by various agencies of the United Nations and the World Wildlife Fund.

The Rutgers University Libraries, the Princeton University Library and the New York Public Library were consulted on many occasions, and the activities and publications of the National Wildlife Federation, the U.S. Wildlife Service, the World Wildlife Fund, the National Audubon Society, the Wilderness Society and the National Parks Association proved useful and stimulating in numerous ways.

I wish to express my appreciation also to the guides, rangers and scientists who assisted me in observing wildlife in northern New England and Canada; in the West Indies and South America; in West, East and South Africa, especially in Senegal and Kenya, Uganda and Tanzania; in India, Japan and the Philippines; and last but not least in our own magnificent North American West.

Princeton, N. J.   E. L. JORDAN

Wildlife Around the Globe

By and large, all the mammalian species which inhabit the earth are known to us; an inventory of the world's major wildlife has been taken, and today's problem is the preservation of our heritage. This heritage has been sadly depleted during the last 150 years, and in order to conserve what is left thousands of national parks, wildlife preserves and sanctuaries have been created on all continents. The most important ones, particularly those in ·which all kinds of mammals can be observed, are described in the following outline.

THE AMERICAS
Canada

The fauna in the national parks of mountainous western Canada consists of black bear, grizzly bear, cougar, Rocky Mountain goat, bighorn sheep, caribou, moose, elk, beaver, and smaller fur bearers. The parks are Banff National Park in Alberta, Glacier National Park in the Selkirk Mountains of British Columbia, Jasper National Park on the eastern slopes of the Canadian Rockies, and Waterton Lakes National Park in southwestern Alberta. Wood Buffalo National Park, a preserve of 17,300 square miles in Alberta and the Northwest Territories between Lake Athabasca and the Great Slave Lake shelters the only remaining large herd of bison (wood buffaloes), more than 10,000 head, in its natural state.

United States

Big Bend National Park on the Mexican border of Texas preserves a variety of desert mammals. Carlsbad Caverns National Park in southeastern New Mexico, the largest known system of caverns in the world, is the home of millions of bats of 11 species which spiral upward from the cave at nightfall like a huge column of smoke. Everglades National Park at the southern tip of Florida, a "river of grass," supports a wealth of wildlife, particularly of birds. The cougar, black bear, manatee and white-tailed deer are also encountered here. The great national parks of our western mountains — Mt. Rainier and Olympic in Washington; Glacier in Montana; Grand Teton in Wyoming; Yellowstone in Wyoming, Montana and Idaho; Rocky Mountain in Colorado; Yosemite, Sequoia and Kings Canyon in California — protect the Rocky Mountain goat, bighorn sheep, moose, elk, mule deer, white-tailed deer, pronghorn antelope, black bear, grizzly bear, pine marten, fisher, wolverine and beaver. Mt. McKinley National Park and 18 preserves in Alaska have a northern fauna including caribou, reindeer (introduced), Dall sheep, moose, grizzly bear, Kodiak brown bear, polar bear, wolf, wolverine, Arctic fox, Rocky Mountain goat, fur seal, sea otter, and whales. Grand Canyon, Crater Lake, Great Smoky Mountains, Acadia (Maine), Hawaii Volcanoes and Haleakala National Parks are famous for their scenery rather than for their wildlife.

Brazil

The Amazon River valley is the largest nature preserve in the world; it is not protected by the state since such a measure is hardly necessary. The area, half the size of Europe, is so huge and so inaccessible that only five percent of it has been mapped; twice every year the Amazon and its 200 tributaries flood the primeval shore forests to a width of 30 miles. The jungle is inhabited by the jaguar, tapir, deer, peccary, howler monkey, and marmoset. The population of birds, reptiles and insects in the Amazon valley is varied and huge.

Ecuador

Galápagos Islands National Park is perhaps the most unique nature preserve in the world. When the Spaniards discovered the islands they marveled at the bleak, black lava rocks, the smoking volcanoes, the man-high fantastic cactus plants, and the throngs of dragon-like, nine-foot lizards; the females black with fiery red spots, the males with light-green jagged giant combs. When their ships were plagued with swishing currents and milky fogs, the Spaniards believed they were at the entrance to Hades and called the islands "Las Encantadas," the enchanted isles. Happily they discovered that the lizards were harmless and that the native giant tortoises (it took eight men to carry one of these "galápagos") furnished excellent meat. More than a hundred years ago Charles Darwin visited the islands and conceived there his theory of evolution; to honor Darwin the government of Ecuador declared the four largest islands — Isabela, Santa Cruz, San Cristóbal, and Floreana — a national park. The British-supported Charles Darwin Research Station on Santa Cruz investigates and studies the islands' flora and fauna.

EUROPE
Finland and Sweden

The northern national parks of Scandinavia protect the pasturage of the reindeer owned by the Lapps. Bear, lynx, wolf, wolverine, moose and fallow deer are encountered there but are not protected. Bird life is abundant.

United Kingdom

Her more than 100 nature preserves are largely bird sanctuaries. Some mammals such as the wildcat, pine marten, red deer and polecat, are protected in Beinn Eighe National Nature Reserve in Ross-shire, Scotland.

France

The Camargue is one of the most spectacular nature preserves in Europe. It is not a national park but to the extent of 58 square miles it is owned by the Societé Nationale d'Acclimatisation de France. It comprises the delta triangle between the two large branches of the Rhône River and includes the coast. Beaches, salt marshes, lagoons and savannas shaded by groves of tamarisk trees form the background for a unique scene. Herds of half-wild horses gallop over the steppe; cowboys on horseback, with long poles, manage herds of steers; herons, gulls, sea swallows and vultures soar above; but the great attraction are the flamingos which breed on the salt marshes by the thousands. Whether these magnificent white birds stand in groups on their long pink legs or rise in a pink-white-red mass flight, they are a sight to behold.

Switzerland

The Swiss National Park is located in the canton of Graubünden (Grisons), on the Italian border, at an elevation of 4,500 to 9,500 feet. It is kept a true wilderness; nothing has been removed or changed. Its fauna includes approximately 1,300 chamois, 200 ibex, 700 deer, marmot, snow hare, marten, fox, weasel, badger and otter. The ibex ("Steinbock" in German) is still looked upon with a certain awe because in Switzerland, Austria and Germany "Steinbock" is the name of the tenth sign of the zodiac, Capricorn. An aura of astrological magic surrounds the animal, and for centuries its horns and blood have been considered a remedy for disease and an antidote for poison.

Italy

Gran Paradiso National Park in northwestern and Stelvio National Park in northeastern Italy shelter chamois, weasel, stone marten, fox, badger, polecat, otter, marmot, Alpine hare, and a few bears. Gran Paradiso is the only wilderness where the indigenous ibex has survived and it is a source from which the Swiss and Austrian reservations have been restocked. Abruzzi National Park, a mountain wilderness in central Italy, contains the Abruzzi bear, chamois, roebuck, weasel, polecat, marten, badger and otter; lynx and wolf are probably extinct there by now.

Białowieza National Park in northeastern Poland is operated together with a contiguous park in the Soviet Union; the international boundary crosses the park. The former hunting preserve of the czars is one of the continent's most famous nature parks because it preserves the rare European bison. In the days of the czars some 2,000 specimens roamed the swampy forests; after the depredations of two world wars the park had to be restocked from remnants in the Caucasus mountains; now some 30 bison live there in a free state while over a hundred are acclimatized in fenced-in plots. Another interesting inhabitant of the park is the wild tarpan horse; moose, brown bear, lynx and beaver are found there also.

Besides the above-mentioned preserve of the European bison the Soviet Union maintains seven national parks and 40 nature preserves. The Caucasus National Park has an abundance of wildlife comprising bear, panther, lynx, badger, otter, wolf, red deer, wild boar, chamois and Caucasian goat. Krimskiy National Park on the Crimean Peninsula consists of mountain forests with herds of red deer and mouflon.

Nineteen national parks on the islands of Honshu and Hokkaido protect the Yezo brown bear, antelopes, monkeys, snow rabbits, the "crying hare," Japanese weasels, Yezo squirrels, seals and the wild horses of Cape Toi (Toi-misaki).

Her great nature preserves like Corbett National Park in Uttar Pradesh state or Hazaribagh National Park in Bihar state are inhabited by large numbers of mammals. Their wildlife includes the elephant, tiger, leopard, sloth bear, wild dog, hyena, wild boar, marten, nilgai, blackbuck, buffalo, gaur, spotted deer, sambhar, goral, Indian gazelle, porcupine and flying squirrel. Many parks and preserves are equipped with observation platforms and have riding elephants available for excursions. In the Kaziranga Sanctuary on the southern bank of the Brahmaputra River a herd of 300 head of the very rare great Indian rhinoceros lives in swamps of thick grass. The famous Gir Sanctuary in western India is the last stronghold of the Asiatic lion; about 300 animals survive. A new lion preserve stocked from the Gir Forest has been established in the Chandraprabha Sanctuary near Varanasi. Wildlife preserves in the Himalaya shelter a number of high-mountain species such as the Himalayan black bear, the snow leopard and the goral.

The six national parks of Thailand and the game preserves of Burma contain approximately the same species of mammals as are found in the tropical sanctuaries in India.

The most unusual of Indonesia's wildlife preserves are Rintja and Padar Nature Parks on small islands east of Java which protect the giant monitor of Komodo, the largest living lizard. About 1,000 of these six-foot dragons survive.

AFRICA
Congo
(Democratic Republic)

Albert National Park is one of the world's famous game preserves. It is a closed unit situated in the Great Rift Valley ("Great African Ditch") which is about 30 miles wide, with walls 3,000 feet tall. The bottom is covered with lakes, forests and savannas which form the grazing ground of huge herds of zebras and antelopes. Lake Edward with its stands of papyrus reeds is the home of thousands of hippos, pelicans, cormorants, ibises, crowned cranes and ospreys. In the mountain forests herds of elephants are found. The southern sector of the park, near Lake Kivu, is the home of the gorilla. In small family groups these huge apes roam the *Hagenia* forests. There, under a roof of light foliage, they wander among the trees with the reddish bark. Their number is estimated at 2,000. One of the rarest animals known is also found here, the okapi. When the first photo of an okapi reached Europe in 1910, it was described as a forest horse with a donkey's ears. Now about 16 are kept in various zoological gardens, but few white men have seen one in its native environment. The only human beings living permanently in this area are the pygmies.

Rhodesia

Its national parks and game preserves are rich in eland, sable antelope, bushbuck, reedbuck, steinbok, oribi, waterbuck, duiker, klipspringer, sitatunga, hippo, buffalo, zebra, wart hog, elephant, rhino, lion and leopard. Victoria Falls National Park surrounds the spectacular cascades of the Zambezi River.

South Africa

Kruger National Park in eastern Transvaal was established by President Kruger in 1892. It is Africa's most famous wildlife sanctuary and occupies almost one-fifth of the territory of Transvaal. More than 1,000 miles of roads and several well-equipped camps are at the disposal of visitors from all continents. Practically every species of South African fauna lives here in its natural habitat; hippos and crocodiles dwell in the park's watery hideouts; herds of elephants roam the bush; giraffes feed on trees in the open forest; and herds of antelopes, gazelles, zebras and other plains animals graze in the veld. Lions are common, leopards are shy and rarely seen, hyenas howl at night, wart hogs wander everywhere, and baboons take rides on the hoods of cruising automobiles. The other preserves of South Africa have similar animal populations.

Tanzania

Serengeti National Park, consisting of 4,450 square miles in northern Tanzania, is an area of open plains, savannas, acacia bush, river-thickets and rocky ridges, at elevations from 3,700 to 7,300 feet. This is the range of the largest remaining assemblage of hoofed animals in Africa, amounting to about 400,000 head; it covers their annual migrations which extend over 300 miles. With these vast herds of wildebeest, zebra, Thomson's gazelle, etc., an exceptionally large number of carnivores is associated — lions, leopards and cheetahs. Controlled hunting areas have been established at the periphery of the park. Ngorongoro Conservation Area in northern Tanzania extends from dry, treeless plains through thornbush, rain forest and bamboo stands to mountain moorland. The plains have the same wildlife as the Serengeti National Park while the fauna on high ground includes rhino, buffalo, elephant, leopard, reedbuck, gnu and the giant forest hog. There are also 135,000 head of the picturesque Masai cattle on the reservation. The scenery is spectacular; the volcanic massif of the Crater Highlands rises over 11,000 feet from the floor of the Great Rift Valley which itself is at an elevation of 3,300 feet.

Nairobi Royal National Park in southwestern Kenya enjoys great popularity with tourists because of its nearness to Nairobi. The park, in sight of the high-rise buildings of Kenya's capital, consists of grasslands and savannas at an elevation of 5,000 to 6,000 feet; it is one of the best-known observation posts of African wildlife, especially of lions, zebras, giraffes and antelopes. Since the park is small, the wildlife populations depend on the contiguous Ngong Reserve for survival. Amboseli National Reserve is situated on the Tanzanian boundary of southern Kenya. The snow-clad peak of Mt. Kilimanjaro, just south, dominates the plains of the reserve. The swamps and springs of the otherwise arid landscape attract large concentrations of wild animals. Motion pictures which use African wildlife as a background are usually filmed here. The important animals of the Reserve are the lion, elephant, rhino, buffalo, zebra and eland.

Murchison Falls National Park in northwestern Uganda includes one of the world's great cascades, also the Victoria Nile with a heavy concentration of crocodiles and hippos. On the open grassy plains the lion, leopard, elephant, rhino, buffalo, and other animals are encountered.

Flinders Chase National Park on Kangaroo Island shelters kangaroos, wallabies, wombats, echidnas, platypuses and koalas. Part of the park is closed to the public to preserve the rare black-faced kangaroo.

Kinglake National Park in south-central Victoria consists of heavily forested mountain country with deep fern gullies and waterfalls. This is the home of the unique lyre bird. Besides birds and reptiles the varied wildlife includes the great gray kangaroo, wombat, black-tailed wallaby, bandicoot, dasyure (Australian native cat), ring-tailed possum, koala, echidna and platypus. Lakes National Park is located on Sperm Whale Peninsula in the Gippsland Lake District. This is a sand dune area rich in bird life; its 410 species include the very rare green and crimson ground parrot. Marsupials are numerous: the great gray kangaroo, the black-tailed wallaby, the rare brush wallaby, the brush-tailed opossum, the ring-tailed opossum, the opossum mouse, phalanger, wombat, echidna and koala.

One famous natural phenomenon that so far does not enjoy special protection is the Great Barrier Reef, a wall of coral 1,250 miles long, off the northeastern coast of Australia. Its myriads of small islands with quiet green lagoons behind the breaking surf and the colorful fishes that swim around the coral banks are a magnificent sight. At low tide a fantastic display of marine life is exposed to view.

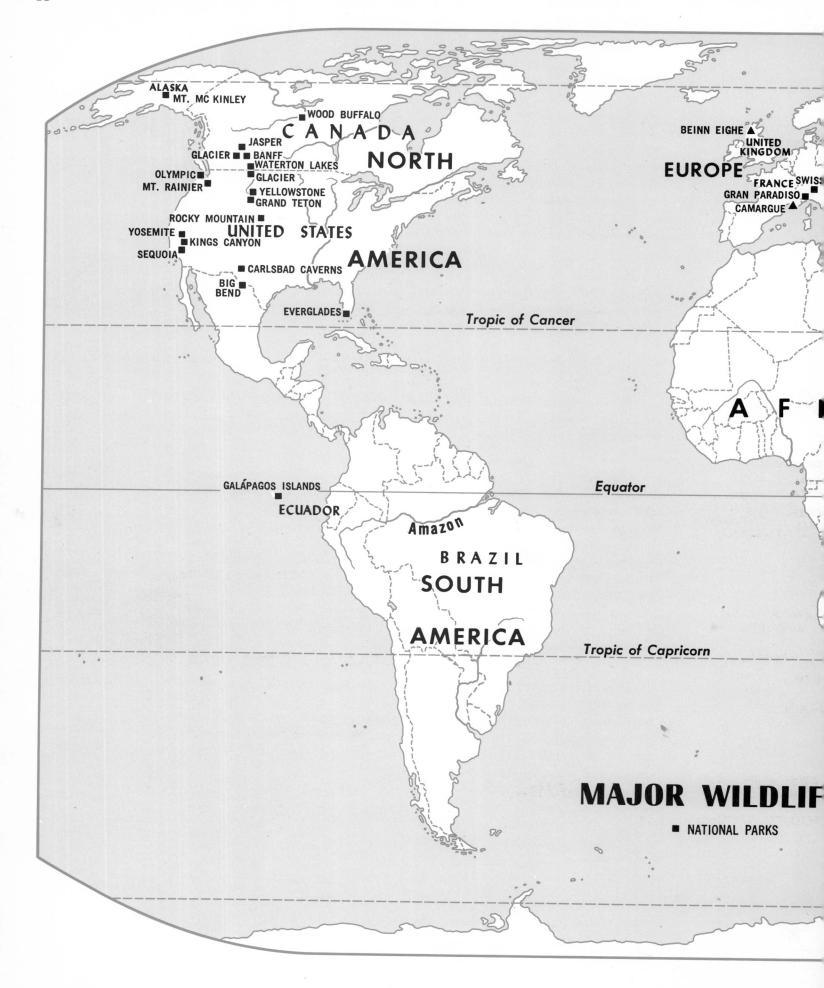

ALASKA
MT. MC KINLEY

WOOD BUFFALO

C A N A D A

NORTH

JASPER
GLACIER BANFF
WATERTON LAKES
OLYMPIC GLACIER
MT. RAINIER
YELLOWSTONE
GRAND TETON

ROCKY MOUNTAIN
YOSEMITE
UNITED STATES
KINGS CANYON
SEQUOIA
AMERICA
CARLSBAD CAVERNS
BIG
BEND
EVERGLADES
Tropic of Cancer

EUROPE

BEINN EIGHE ▲
UNITED
KINGDOM

FRANCE SWISS
GRAN PARADISO
CAMARGUE ▲

A F R

GALÁPAGOS ISLANDS
ECUADOR
Equator

Amazon

B R A Z I L

SOUTH

AMERICA
Tropic of Capricorn

MAJOR WILDLIF

■ NATIONAL PARKS

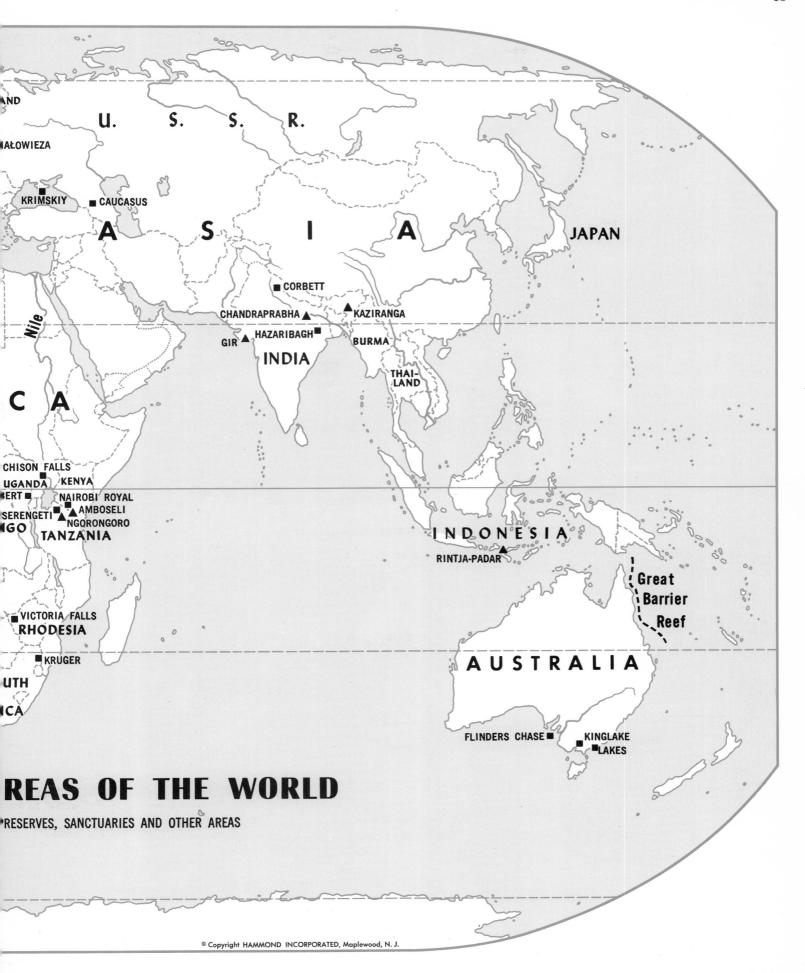

U. S. S. R.

ASIA

JAPAN

AND

ŁOWIEZA

■ KRIMSKIY   ■ CAUCASUS

A   I   A

Nile

■ CORBETT

CHANDRAPRABHA ▲   ▲ KAZIRANGA

GIR ▲   HAZARIBAGH ■

BURMA

INDIA

THAI-
LAND

C A

CHISON FALLS

UGANDA   KENYA

ERT ■

■ NAIROBI ROYAL

SERENGETI ■   ▲ AMBOSELI

GO   ▲ NGORONGORO

TANZANIA

INDONESIA

RINTJA-PADAR ▲

Great
Barrier
Reef

■ VICTORIA FALLS

RHODESIA

AUSTRALIA

KRUGER

UTH

ICA

FLINDERS CHASE ■   ■ KINGLAKE
                    ■ LAKES

REAS OF THE WORLD

RESERVES, SANCTUARIES AND OTHER AREAS

The Most Ancient Orders

EGG-LAYERS — MONOTREMATA

The egg-laying mammals of Australia, Tasmania and New Guinea include the spiny anteaters and the duck-billed platypuses which have a unique method of reproduction. They lay eggs which are hatched outside of the female's body. Some of their features are typical for mammals while others are similar to those of reptiles. Like mammals they grow hair and have mammary glands, with milk trickling from a pair of areas where it is licked up by the young. They are considered warm-blooded although their body temperature is low. Their carriage, on the other hand, is like that of reptiles; their eggs are rubbery with plastic shells like those of snakes and turtles, and their bone structure has several reptilian features. They represent a separate line of evolution but indicate the development of reptiles into mammals.

POUCHED MAMMALS — MARSUPIALIA

The pouched mammals comprise eight living families of diverse types; some live in trees, some on the ground, others in burrows. Some are meat-eaters, others insect-eaters and still others vegetarians. Even the pouch shows a great variety of forms; mostly it opens to the front but in some species it points to the rear; it may be a large bag or a shelf-like flap of skin, or it may be merely vestigial. Marsupials have an unusually short gestation period so that their young are little more than half-grown embryos at birth. From the mother's body they are ejected at the base of the tail; from there they crawl along a furry path into their mother's pouch where they attach themselves to a nipple. As they grow older they release the teat but still remain in the pouch. Even after they begin to venture into the outside world they hurry back to the sheltering pouch when they are frightened. Marsupials represent Australia's native fauna; they flourished as long as the continent remained detached from western civilization; but many marsupial species have become extinct since such predatory animals as dogs, cats and foxes were introduced by immigrants, and such large-scale consumers of grass as sheep and rabbits.

INSECT-EATERS — INSECTIVORA

The insect-eaters, comprising eight living families, live in untold millions throughout the world except in Australia, the polar regions, and the larger part of South America. These small mammals with narrow snouts and five-digit claws on each limb are terrestrial or semi-aquatic, and some are burrowers. Their ears and eyes are small, and the eyes of some insectivores have no opening on the outside. They have no weapons with which to defend themselves but survive because they are nocturnal and hide in crevices, deserted burrows or the dense vegetation of deep forests; some spend their whole lives underground. The most primitive members of the order are thought to be similar to the basic stock from which certain lines of mammals have developed.

Spiny Anteater

Tachyglossus aculeatus

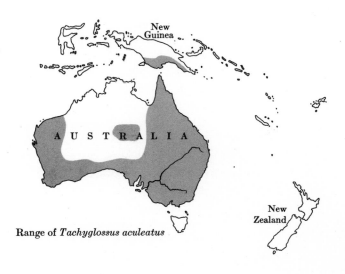

Range of *Tachyglossus aculeatus*

AN EGG-LAYER THAT SUCKLES HER YOUNG. The female of this strange species develops a temporary pouch during the breeding season; there she raises her young, but how her single egg (rarely two or three eggs) travels from her body into the pouch is not known. The tiny naked young, less than half an inch long, licks the yellowish milk which runs through various ducts into the pouch. After six to eight weeks the young is released and deposited at a sheltered spot. It has the prospect of a long life; in captivity one specimen lived for 50 years. The spiny anteater, also called echidna, has a head-and-body length of up to 20 inches and a weight of up to 20 pounds. Its brown or black body fur is intermixed with barbless spines of yellowish color. The strong curved claws are excellent digging tools, and in case of danger the echidna rapidly digs straight down, with all four claws, until it disappears in the ground with merely a dome of spines confronting the discouraged attacker. It also can roll itself into a ball of spines, with the same effect. The elongated second toe of its hind foot serves as a fur cleaver and skin scratcher. With its long, sticky tongue it catches worms and insects, and since it does not possess any teeth it grinds its food between the bony ridges of its tongue and those of its palate. For most of the day it likes to retreat to crevices in rocky terrain, and if it wedges itself in an opening it is almost impossible to remove it.

BIRD, REPTILE OR MAMMAL? This puzzling creature with a beaver tail and a duck bill follows the most unusual reproductive method: after an elaborate courtship the female lays two (rarely one or three) eggs whose pliable shells resemble those of reptiles; she hatches them in a nesting burrow dug into a riverbank for a length of up to 60 feet. Her young lap up the milk which flows through pores into the fur of her underbelly. The male possesses a dangerous weapon: the spurs of its hind legs are connected with venom glands the poison from which can kill a small animal and cause pain and swelling on human limbs. A native of the lakes and streams of eastern Australia and Tasmania, an adult specimen will reach a length of up to a foot and a half and a weight of up to 4½ pounds. It eagerly dives and digs for snails, shrimps, small fish and worms to still its ravenous appetite; in captivity it will eat about half of its weight in food every day.

Range of *Ornithorhynchus anatinus*

Duck-billed Platypus

Ornithorhynchus anatinus

American Opossum

Didelphis marsupialis

Range of
Didelphis marsupialis

PLAYING POSSUM. This pictorial phrase has become part of the American imagery; for feigning death as a means of surviving a dangerous situation has also human applications. A few other animals use the same ruse but the opossum does it convincingly, with body curled and limbs limp; it is a reaction of the nervous system resembling a fainting spell. Folklore asserts that opossums mate through the nose and that the female blows her young into her pouch; these are fables. The tiny young, the size of a bee, attach themselves to the 13 nipples in their mother's pouch and stay there for 60 to 70 days; then they emerge and for a few weeks use their mother's body as a playground on which they move about freely. The American opossum has a head-and-body length of up to 19½ inches and a weight of up to 12 pounds. Its underfur, mostly gray, reddish and black, is mixed with white-tipped guard hairs. Its range extends from northern Argentina to southern Canada. This represents an enormous northern extension which occurred since the European settlement. The opossum, tough and resilient, survives the hard northern winters although its naked tail often suffers from frostbite. Omnivorous, it looks for animal and vegetable matter mainly on the ground but also climbs trees.

A MISTAKE OF NATURE? The litters of the Australian "native cat" are large; cases of 18 to 24 young have been recorded. But the shallow pouch of the female is equipped with only six nipples, and by necessity many of the young die; usually only four to eight survive. They open their eyes after approximately 11 weeks and emerge from the pouch in about 15 weeks, getting accustomed to meat but also continuing their suckling. After four to four and one-half months they gain independence. These cats, with a head-and-body length of up to 17½ inches and a weight of up to 2½ pounds, occur in two color phases, one black with white spots, the other grayish-brownish with cream-colored spots. The tip of the tail is usually white. They live in the dense forest and on open plains, often in the neighborhood of farm buildings, in southeastern Australia where they are rare and in Tasmania where they are quite common. They spend their days in rocky shelters which sometimes are laid out with grass and bark; there they sleep rolled up in a ball. At night they hunt and devour snakes, frogs, mice, rabbits — any animal they are able to overpower.

Range of *Dasyurus quoll*

Australian "Native Cat"

Dasyurus quoll

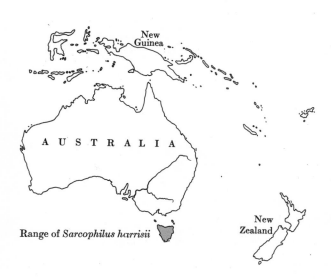

Range of *Sarcophilus harrisii*

Tasmanian Devil

Sarcophilus harrisii

WHY "DEVIL"? Why has such an unusual name been given to this small animal? Apparently the people of Tasmania regard it with a mixture of annoyance and good-natured admiration. They are annoyed because it kills their sheep, small dogs, and poultry, but they acknowledge the courage with which it attacks animals larger than itself and the thoroughness with which it finishes its meal; its splendid bone-crusher teeth set in a massive skull grind down meat, bones, fur and feathers. It has also a few other characteristics which may seem "devilish:" it kills and eats the poisonous black tiger snake without being harmed. It is vicious and ill-tempered when someone disturbs it, and when two devils fight each other their teeth clash and their throats growl and snarl. Living in the dense thickets of the island of Tasmania, the male reaches a head-and-body length of approximately 2½ feet with a weight of 20 pounds while the female is considerably smaller. Its fur is dark brown or black, with irregular white patches on the throat and rump; the snout is also white, with a pinkish hue. The animal hunts at night and retreats during the day although it sometimes emerges for a sunbath. Cavities in rocks, roots or logs are used as shelter and are provided with a nest of bark and vegetable matter. There the female raises her young, usually two, in a completely closed pouch with four teats; the babies hold on to them for about 15 weeks, then emerge with eyes open and fur complete. But they continue to suckle for several months. They will live to an age of approximately eight years.

Tasmanian "Wolf"

Thylacinus cynocephalus

THE POUCHED DOG WITH A WOLF'S HEAD.
That is the translation of the scientific name of this largest of the marsupial carnivores. Its story is tragic: When Tasmania was settled, the farmers killed this "wolf" at sight because it attacked their livestock, and the settlers' dogs seem to have hunted it down on their own forays. After the apparently last living individual was shot in 1930, several scientific expeditions tried to determine whether the Tasmanian wolf is still a living species in its natural environment. Apparently it is, although not more than several specimens may be alive. In the mountainous parts of western Tasmania, in a roadless uninhabited wilderness tracks have been seen and one "wolf" was actually observed in its own habitat in 1961. The few that are left hunt like real wolves in small family groups, or singly or in pairs, pursuing their prey indefatigably until it is exhausted and surrenders. The "wolf" is most interested in the victim's blood, and at the act of killing usually bites through the jugular vein and sucks the blood. Kangaroos and wallabys are its principal food but it also kills birds and small mammals. Its head-and-body length reaches 4 feet 3 inches; its short coarse fur is tawny or brownish yellow on the back, with a design of 13 to 19 dark brown bands which stand out strongly at the tail and fade toward the head. Its jaws have an unusually wide gap, said to reach almost 180 degrees; the pouch of the female, with two teats, points backwards. The days are spent in a rocky shelter or hollow trunk and the hunting is done at night.

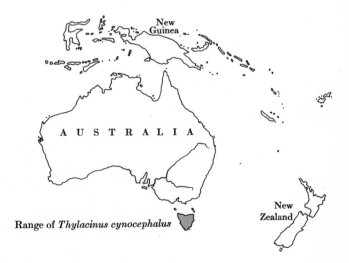

Range of *Thylacinus cynocephalus*

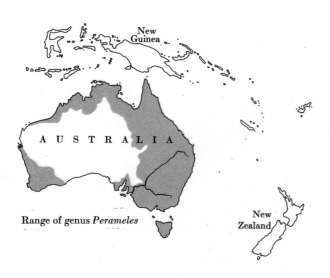

Range of genus *Perameles*

Eastern Barred Bandicoot

Perameles fasciata

A MARSUPIAL NAMED AFTER A MAMMAL. A large rodent native to India and Ceylon is called *bandicota*, meaning "pig-rat" in one of the area's local languages. How and why this name was transferred to the Australian marsupial is not certain, but it is assumed that it was done at sometime during the 18th century by the explorer Bass in whose honor Bass Strait between Australia and Tasmania was named. The marsupial bandicoot family includes a variety of species, measuring in size from 6¾ to 21½ inches. Most of them have hands with five fingers and sharp nails for digging, a non-prehensile tail and a long nose with which they root in the ground. They are nocturnal feeders with a mixed animal-plant diet; their liquid requirements are very low; they seem to be satisfied with licking the dew from the plants. They inhabit almost any kind of terrain including forests, river banks, areas near human settlements and in New Guinea even mountains up to a height of 13,000 feet. Their range includes, besides New Guinea, Australia, Tasmania, and islands in various South Sea archipelagos. On the ground they move at a lively pace, sometimes with a kind of gallop. With the exception of one genus (*Thylacomys*) which digs burrows, they build nests of grass on the surface; there they raise their young, usually two to six. In Australia they are protected by law; however, the natives hunt and eat them.

A WILDLIFE COLORAMA. One peculiarity of the genus *Cuscus* is the multiplicity of colors in which their woolly fur appears; it ranges from white to black, with reddish, brown and gray as intermediate shades. Of the spotted cuscus only the adult male is spotted, and sometimes it is white without spots. The female's coat is plain; the young change color several times as they grow up, and adults are said to do so for the breeding season. Their big eyes have a yellow rim, and bright yellow is the color of their noses. A musky odor emerges from the body when it is stroked. Their prehensile tails, covered with scales at the end, and their strong, curved claws are useful in the arboreal life they lead; occasionally they climb down to the forest floor. By day they curl up for a rest, at a protected spot, and at night they hunt for insects and small birds; they also eat leaves, fruits, and eggs. These one- to two-foot-long marsupials are found on the Australian continent in Queensland, in the Cape York area; on the large islands of New Guinea, Timor, and Celebes; and on numerous small ones in the Bismarck and Solomon archipelagos. The pouch of the female contains four nipples but the number of young is only one or two. In New Guinea the aborigines hunt and eat cuscus; besides, the python snakes catch the slow-moving animals and kill and devour considerable numbers of them.

Spotted Cuscus

Phalanger maculatus

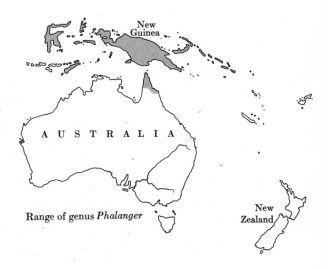

Range of genus *Phalanger*

Flying Phalanger

Petaurus breviceps

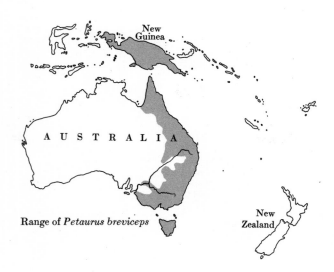

Range of *Petaurus breviceps*

THE MOST COMMON MARSUPIAL. The name of this widely distributed Australian mammal refers to its "phalanges," i.e., its finger-and-toe bones which are constructed for climbing. In 1770 Captain Cook named these creatures "opossum" but today only the expression "possum" survives, to distinguish them from the American "opossum." Pictured here is the lesser gliding possum, a phalanger of eastern Australia. This extremely lively small animal with a silky grayish fur, about a foot long and weighing up to 4½ ounces, has gliding membranes with which it covers distances of up to 175 feet. Its food consists of insects, larvae, birds, blossoms and other plant material. The one to three young stay with their parents for several seasons so that as many as a dozen of these animals may live in one nest.

A LIVING TOY. This charming little marsupial with bright, startled eyes, a leathery nose and fluffy ears seems to be the original model of the Teddy Bear. When it has become accustomed to a person it is most trusting and affectionate and puts its arms around the friend's neck. Some of its habits are hilarious; the mother, for instance, will take her naughty baby from her back, put it on her knees and spank it with her flat hand while the youngster screams pitifully. In spite of these endearing qualities it is almost impossible to keep a koala as a pet because it needs the leaves of 12 species of eucalyptus trees for its nourishment. Each type of tree has a certain essential oil in its leaves only part of the year, and the koala knows when to change from one species to another. Its original range are the eucalyptus forests of Australia where it was slaughtered to near-extinction because of its warm, lovely gray fur. But today it is not only fully protected but also re-established at various locations in New South Wales, Queensland and Victoria, and its numbers are increasing rapidly. An adult male will reach a length of 33 inches and a weight of up to 33 pounds. The single young will stay in its mother's pouch for half a year and ride on her back for another half year; it is weaned by eating food pre-digested by its mother.

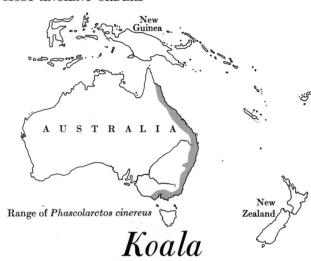

Range of *Phascolarctos cinereus*

Koala

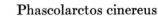

Phascolarctos cinereus

Wombat

Phascolomis ursinus

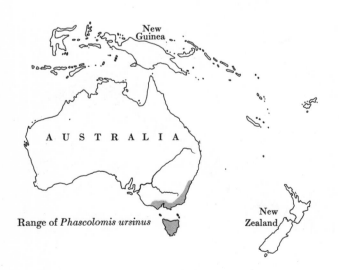

Range of *Phascolomis ursinus*

A SMALL POUCHED BEAR. The wombat's range comprises southeastern Australia where it lives in the hills and mountain chains of the coast; it occurs also on the island of Tasmania. Once upon a time it was a common animal on the islands of Bass Strait, between the Australian mainland and Tasmania; according to local tradition quite a number of wombats had been tamed by fishermen on King Island and served as playful pets, feeding in the woods but returning to their masters every night and sharing the native huts. Today, however, the animal is extinct on the islands, except on Flinders where it survives. Although the wombat looks like a small bear, its dental arrangements are rodent-like; its teeth, including two upper and two lower front teeth, are rootless and grow continually. An adult wombat may reach a head-and-body length of not quite 4 feet and a weight of up to 78 pounds; the color of its coarse fur varies, ranging from yellowish and gray to dark brown and black. It uses its hind feet as a weapon, kicking both of them vigorously when touched, and its front feet to tear loose the seed stems of which it is fond; roots and grass are also consumed. Being a powerful digger it excavates extended burrows with a leaf-and-bark-lined nest; there the female raises her single young. Her pouch contains two teats and points backwards. Its life span is quite long; in captivity one specimen lived for 26 years.

A LIVELY SMALL KANGAROO. The red-necked wallaby belongs to the genus *Wallabia*, the brush or scrub wallabies whose 11 species live in Australia, Tasmania, New Guinea and several small islands. Their habitat is not only the brush and scrub country but also the open forest. They are well adapted to the climate and in periods of drought seem to find the water they need by eating juicy roots. In head-and-body length and weight they vary considerably, from 1 foot 1 inch to 3 feet 5 inches, and from 8¾ pounds to 53 pounds in weight. The coloration ranges from pale sandy and reddish to dark gray. The species illustrated here is called *rufogrisea* because of its red neck and shoulders. The species *agilis* has been named for its agility; it is probably the fastest representative of the kangaroo family. The species *elegans*, the "pretty-faced wallaby," has a handsome face of various light and dark color tones. The tail serves as a solid prop for all species. The wallabies have one habit in common with other marsupials: when the weather is hot or they are in a state of excitement they vigorously lick their forearms and hands; in this way body heat is released which affords some relief. During the warm midday hours they retreat to a shady cover; they like to graze or browse in the morning and late afternoon. The cattlemen and sheep ranchers consider them a pest, because of their appetite for grass, and large numbers are killed. They are persecuted also for their hide; thousands are trapped and their skins are exported since luxury goods of wallaby leather are in fashion. In some areas they have been reduced to a point where the danger of extinction exists.

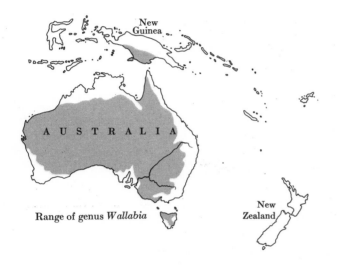

Range of genus *Wallabia*

Red-necked Wallaby

Wallabia rufogrisea

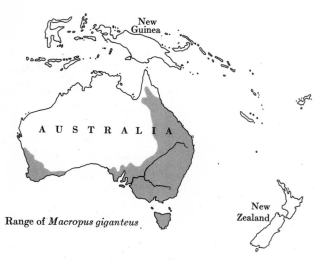

Range of *Macropus giganteus*

A "MOB" LED BY A "BOOMER." Since the kangaroo has become a symbol of Australia, the Australians have bestowed several good-natured nicknames on their best-known native animals. A herd sometimes numbering several hundred is called "a mob," and the old males who keep order in the flock are "the boomers." The bluish-gray females of the wallaroo species are called "blue flyers." Three species live in Australia and Tasmania; the great gray kangaroo which is pictured here dwells in the forest and bush sections; the red kangaroo inhabits the inland plains, and the wallaroo prefers the mountain ranges. These largest marsupials attain a head-and-body length of 4½ feet, plus a tail of approximately 3½ feet; their weight

Great Gray Kangaroo

Macropus giganteus

Range of *Dendrolagus bennettianus*

Tree Kangaroo

Dendrolagus bennettianus

reaches 155 pounds; since their growth process continues throughout life, the oldest specimens are the biggest. The coarse fur has color shades from red and brown to gray and black. They move in leaps of up to six feet when at leisure and may jump up to 30 feet when rushed. Their so-called "five-footed gait" involves their hind legs for the jump and their arms and tail for balancing. They graze or browse and are well accustomed to the dry climate; for long periods they exist without water. In cavernous shelters with a cool temperature they do not need any water at all.

ANTICS IN THE TREETOPS. To watch these agile small kangaroos is entertaining. Speedily they travel from tree to tree, sometimes jumping from a high treetop to a lower one, in a daring leap of 30 feet. Among the branches they rest in small groups, feed on leaves and fruits, and mate. Sometimes they descend to the ground; if in a hurry, they negotiate jumps of 60 feet without injury. Otherwise they descend by backing down. On the ground they move with a characteristic posture; the tail forms an upward arch as they leap along, and in counterbalance the body bends forward. They live in rather inaccessible wooded areas, five species in New Guinea and two in northeastern Queensland. Their head-and-body length is about 2½ feet; their long, furry tail of over 3 feet serves as a brace; it is not prehensile. The coloration varies in the different species; reddish, brown and blackish tones predominate. The natives hunt them: one man climbs a tree whereupon the animal jumps down into the arms of the hunter's accomplice. Pictured here is the dusky or Bennet's tree kangaroo.

Long-tailed Shrew

Sorex cinereus

A RESTLESS SEARCHER. This nervous little animal is busily rushing about, day and night, summer and winter, in search of insects, worms, carrion and plant matter; but the long-held belief that it requires its own weight in food every day is doubted now, following recent experiments. It enjoys short stretches of deep sleep but when awake it restlessly travels through tunnels and over runways of its own making, or over those of mice and moles; its slender, highly mobile snout rotates constantly. The genus of the long-tailed shrews comprises 40 species; in the New World their range extends northward from Central America, and in the Old World northward from a line stretching from Israel through Iran and Afghanistan to Burma; they live in wooded or scrubby moist areas, including tundras. In length they vary from 1¾ to 3¾ inches, their tails adding 1 to 3¼ inches, and they weigh 3 to 16 grams. Their sleek tan-to-black fur is either uniform or combines two or three color tones. They live solitary lives, emitting high-pitched squeaky noises when scurrying about or angrily fighting competitors. They fashion a nest of vegetable matter in the shape of a ball; there two to ten young are born and weaned in three weeks. After that they begin their independent short life which lasts generally for about one year, at the most two years.

Range of *Sorex cinereus*

A WELL-ORGANIZED UNDERGROUND. The moles of Europe and Asia hardly ever see the light of day; they are perfectly equipped for underground life. Their strong, flesh-colored feet are turned outward and are broader than long. The limbs are short and appear even shorter because the body skin is fastened around ankles and wrists. These moles dig with all four feet and occasionally push up a vent to dispose of the surplus soil; the result is the molehill typical of European pastures. Their underground homes consist of two circular tunnels at different depths, a nest at a central location, and connecting and radiating passageways. Their eyes are hidden under the fur because they hardly need them, and when they run backward instead of forward the hairs of their fur turn over to the other side. Their search for food goes on day and night, and a mole not fed for 12 hours will die of starvation. Their food consists of insects, worms, and other small animals. Sometimes they store worms; by biting off the latters' front segments they prevent the captives from burrowing their way out. The four species of this genus live in most of the area of Eurasia, with the exception of the Arctic regions and of the Central Asian mountain plateaus. They attain a length of up to 7 inches and a weight of up to 120 grams. The velvety fur of these moles is usually gray but there are variations in color from whitish to golden to black, sometimes with irregular patches.

Range of genus *Talpa*

Eurasian Mole

Talpa europaea

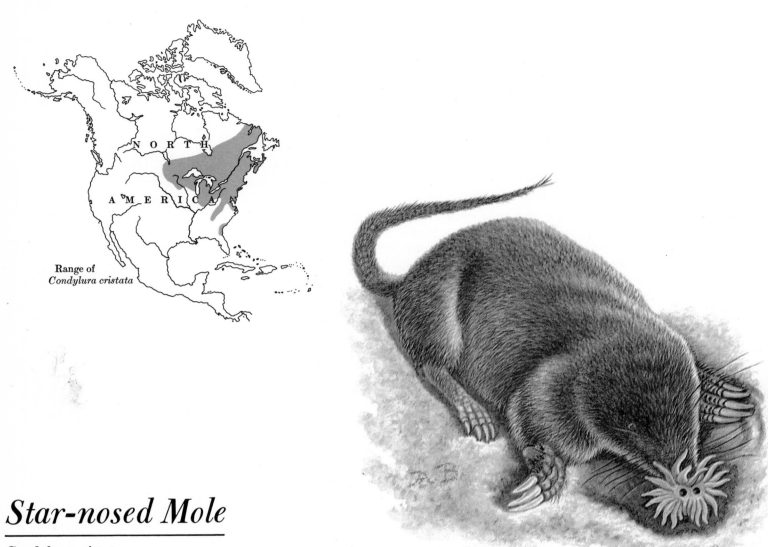

Range of
Condylura cristata

Star-nosed Mole

Condylura cristata

TWENTY-TWO FINGERS SURROUND ITS SNOUT. This is one of the strangest creatures of America's fauna; for a flesh-colored flower seems to be placed on top of its muzzle, a ring of 22 fingers which aid in the mole's search for food. Two upper tentacles point straight ahead, the others vibrate. This pink star, a pronounced mark already at birth, together with tiny eyes and relatively huge paddle-shaped hands give this mole a highly individualistic appearance. Another unusual feature is the storing of fat in the tail; in early spring at the approach of breeding time the tails of both the male and the female grow in diameter, apparently a build-up of strength. The tail is covered with scales and is thinner at the base than in the middle. The mole's waterproof fur is black with brown hues; an adult's head-and-body length may reach 5 inches, with a weight of one-fifth of a pound. The species lives in temperate to cold climates, its range extending throughout eastern North America, from Minnesota to Georgia in the south and from Labrador to Manitoba in the north. Damp and wet ground is the preferred environment; there these moles build underground structures of considerable size. Their regular tunnels do not appear as ridges above ground but their deep tunnels produce surface mounds. A number of specimens may set up communal living in connecting tunnel structures. They remain active throughout the winter and do not mind pushing their way through the snow or proceeding under the ice. In brooks and ponds they swim with ease and dive to the bottom for worms, small fish, insects and similar food. They build a nest of grass and leaves where they raise their young; two to seven are born in spring, and weaned in three weeks; the moles begin to breed at the age of ten months.

Gliders and Flyers

"FLYING" LEMURS — DERMOPTERA

The order *Dermoptera* contains only one family and two species which live in the forests and coconut groves of Southeast Asia. These mammals are nearly helpless on the ground; they live in trees and move about by climbing and gliding, not flying. With their sharp recurved claws they ascend a tree, then glide down on a large membrane that extends from the sides of the body to fingers, toes and tail. During the day the lemurs rest, hanging head up with their four claws clinging to a branch, or they are suspended from their hind claws, upside down. Toward evening they glide to their feeding areas, over distances of up to 136 yards; there they eat leaves and buds, flowers and fruits. The single young of the lemur clings to the belly and nipples of its mother.

BATS — CHIROPTERA

The bats of the order *Chiroptera* are the flying mammals. With two suborders, 17 families and about 180 genera they are the second largest order of mammals, surpassed in the number of species only by the rodents. They occur in the temperate and tropical regions of the earth, varying in size from 1 to 16 inches. Their wings are extensions of the skin of back and stomach, consisting of two layers of membrane; with legs and wings in coordinated movements, the bats actually "swim" through the air. Their fur is dense and silky and most of them emit a musky odor from scent glands. In general they do not orient themselves by eyesight but by echolocation; the bat produces certain sounds, usually not audible to humans, and listens to their echo; in that fashion it flies around obstacles and spots insects in flight. When its ears are plugged it loses its way. During the day bats retire to caves, trees and buildings where they hang from ledges and rafters head down. At night they feed on a great variety of diets. The majority live on insects which they catch while in flight. One tropical group which includes the big flying fox feeds on fruits and other vegetation. The flower-feeding species live on nectar and pollen and are tropical and subtropical. Vampire bats suck blood from a tiny incision on the skin of a sleeping animal; their bite may cause rabies and other virus diseases. The carnivorous bats kill and eat small mammals, birds and frogs. The fish-eating bats have strong claws with which they snatch fish from the surface of the water. In the cooler regions bats hibernate in a semitorpid condition, with many life functions suspended. The females bear only a single young each year but the order has a long life-span; in captivity bats have lived for 17 years. On the whole bats are useful since they kill large numbers of insect pests; they also pollinate flowering plants.

Range of *Cynocephalus variegatus*

"Flying" Lemur

Cynocephalus variegatus

LOCOMOTION BY CLIMBING AND GLIDING. **On** the ground where it is practically immobilized, the lemur will look for any tree or object it can climb; it does so skillfully but slowly and is difficult to spot on the tree trunks and branches; for the brownish tones of the male and the grayish ones of the female fur, together with an irregular sprinkling of whitish spots, create a kind of mimicry. When setting out to feed, at dusk, its relatively huge membranes, fastened to the sides of the body, the fingertips, toes and tail, make glides of 450 feet possible. It has a head-and-body length of up to 16½ inches, with a weight of about 4 pounds; living in forests and also in groves of coco palms, its range extends approximately from southern Indochina to Indonesia. It spends its days hanging from its claws in a hollow tree, in a vertical position, and glides to its feeding locations at dusk. Its diet consists of leaves and other green vegetable matter. A single young, sometimes two, attaches

itself to its mother's nipple; two nipples are located almost in her armpits. Because of the lemurs' unique anatomical features, some of them primitive, the two species are treated as a special order.

LONG-DISTANCE FLYER ON A LIQUID DIET. The members of the large family of flying foxes or Old World fruit bats — there are some 130 species — drink fruit juice as their only nourishment. Therefore they have to live in the tropics where fruits are ripening throughout the year, and the larger varieties have to be persevering flyers to reach their food supply. As to the first point, they are found in most of the tropical areas of the Old World, excepting the African continent although they inhabit some small islands near the East African coast. As to the second point, some large varieties are said to commute to feeding

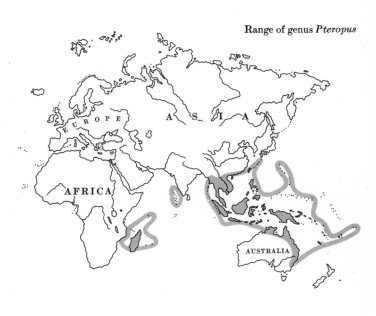

Range of genus *Pteropus*

Flying "Fox"

Pteropus vampyrus

places as far away as 20 miles, sometimes from island to island, and one flying fox has been recorded as landing on a ship 200 miles away from shore. The biggest members of the family have a length of approximately 16 inches with a weight of 2 pounds but a remarkable wing spread of 5 feet. Their coloration is brown or black, in many cases with a yellowish collar between the shoulders. At dusk they set out for groves of fruit trees where they suck the juice but spit out the pulp, unless it is very soft. Aromatic eucalyptus leaves are also a source of juice and pollen. Some bats have been observed drinking sea water on their travels, apparently to provide the needed minerals. They do some damage to orchards although wild fruits are their mainstay. During the day they hang in roosting trees by the hundreds, shoving each other for space. Although the body of these bats has a strong odor, the natives enjoy their flesh and recommend their fat as a medicine.

Vampire Bat

Desmodus rotundus

Range of
Desmodus rotundus

THE ONLY PARASITE AMONG THE MAMMALS OF THE WORLD. The vampire bat feeds on the blood of other living mammals, notably horses, burros, cattle and human beings; however, any warm-blooded animal may be attacked. The bite is painless and relatively little blood is lost, but often it is smeared on the body of the victim and presents a rather gruesome appearance. Consequently the vampire bat has been linked with ancient European myths and ghost stories. The facts are simple; after dark the bats leave their roost and in a silent low-level flight, about three feet above the ground, they land near the intended victim. They jump on the animal and with their chisel-shaped incisor teeth scoop out a piece of skin; then they lap the blood with the tongue. The blood donor is in danger of infection; vampire bats may transmit rabies and various cattle diseases, and the wound may be infected with larvae and bacteria. These bites often cause serious damage to herds of cattle. The range of the vampire bat extends from northern Mexico south to central Chile and Argentina and Uruguay. There the bats live in caves, hollow trees or abandoned buildings. The head-and-body length of an adult is 3½ inches, with a weight of 1½ ounces; the vampire bat's coloration is dark grayish-brown, with light underparts.

The Restless Tribe

MONKEYS, APES, MAN AND RELATIVES — PRIMATES

This order consists of 11 families and more than 60 genera which show extreme differences in size, ranging from the pygmy marmoset with a head-and-body length of 5½ inches and a weight of 2½ ounces to the gorilla which grows to a height of 6 feet and may weigh 610 pounds. The tropical and semi-tropical regions of Africa, Asia, and the Americas are the order's range although the most numerous species, *Homo sapiens,* has adapted himself to almost any region on earth. The most characteristic feature of the primates is the development of the hand (when food is taken to the mouth rather than the mouth lowered to grasp the food, the sense organs remain free and alert) and of the brain. Some monkeys of the New World possess prehensile tails with functions similar to those of hands while the apes and man have no tails. Some primates observe certain periods of intense sexual activity; Old World baboons, for instance, show a great swelling of their highly-colored buttock patches, at that time. But many primates including man have no breeding season and mate at any time of the year. All female members of the order, with the only exception of the tree shrews, have two nipples and mammary glands, usually on the chest. Normally one young is born and develops rather slowly; the longest development period, slower than that of any other creature on earth, is that of man. Baby monkeys hold on to the underfur of their mothers for several months or ride on her or the father's back.

The most important family of the order is that of the *Hominidae* which traditionally is divided into three main stocks, in accordance with color of skin, texture of the hair and features of the face: the Caucasoids who originated in Europe and western Asia; the Negroids of Africa; and the Mongoloids of eastern Asia. The Australian natives, the Australoids, are sometimes regarded as a separate stock, as are the Bushman-Hottentot group. The American Indians and the Eskimos are descendants of Mongoloid tribes which crossed from Asia to North America via the Bering Strait in prehistoric times.

The distinguishing features of *Homo sapiens,* not found in the other primates, are his hairless body, his upright posture and the growth of his brain which made it possible for him to develop a language, to reason and to create what is called a "civilization," although much of his physical strength and of the sharpness of his senses has been lost in the process. The use of heat-producing fire and warm clothing has adapted him to any climate; his ability to travel on land, on water and in the air has given him an unmatched mobility; and his inventiveness in artificially increasing the food supply has resulted in a numerical growth of the species that is currently causing alarm.

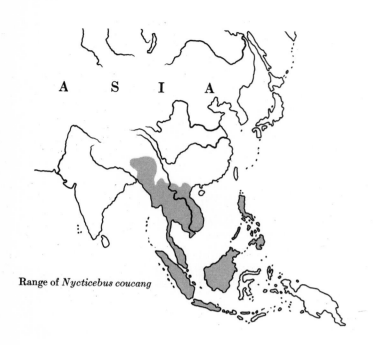

Range of *Nycticebus coucang*

Slow Loris

Nycticebus coucang

A SMALL CLOWN. When the Dutch colonized Indonesia, they called this amusing little native *loeris* which means "clown"; in the form of "loris" the name spread to the animal's whole range of Assam, Indonesia, Southeast Asia, and the Philippines. The nickname seems justified; slowly the loris travels along, carefully placing one hand over the other and proceeding on the underside of a branch just as comfortably as on the upper side. When it sleeps by day, it tucks its head and hands under its thighs and forms a round ball. When foraging at night, it uses two techniques: For securing plant material it hangs head down on a limb by its feet and collects fruits and leaves with its hands; for catching small mammals and insects it stalks its prey silently, then pounces suddenly. It has its own method of washing its hands: It urinates on them. Its thick fur in various shades of brown, reddish, and gray, often with a dorsal stripe in the middle, has a so-called "silver wash," i.e., many hairs are lightly tipped, producing a special sheen. Its thumbs and great toes are attached to the hands and feet at right angles so that their grip firmly clenches the branch. Awed by these peculiar features, the natives have bestowed magical-mystic powers on the slow loris and consider it a demon. This Asiatic animal grows to a length of 15 inches and a weight of 3½ pounds.

A BIG-EYED ACROBAT. Enormous staring eyes are the outstanding feature of this strange creature; these eyes appear as two almost complete circles closely set together and look straight ahead; the eyeballs have a diameter of about two-thirds of an inch. To increase their usefulness, the tarsier can turn its head for nearly 360 degrees, which affords an unusually extensive field of vision. Its membranous, almost naked, ears are always moving. It catches its prey with both hands and chews it while sitting erect; insects are preferred but small reptiles and crustaceans are also welcome. At the tips of its fingers and toes it has fleshy pads which will attach themselves to any kind of surface. Because of its elongated ankle bones (tarsae) it is called tarsier. During the day it sleeps but during the night it performs its lively antics in trees and bushes. It walks on all fours or leaps like a frog, with jumps on the ground of up to five and one-half feet. Tarsiers breed throughout the year; they do not seem to build nests but during the courtship period male and female never tire of cleaning, brushing and grooming each other affectionately. Their single young attaches itself to the mother's underside or is held in her mouth. As in the case of the slow loris, the natives have surrounded this amusing primate with various superstitions. With a head-and-body length of up to 6½ inches, it has a weight of about one-third of a pound; the silky hair has a grayish to brown coloration. Its range comprises Indonesia, the Philippines, and a number of small islands in that general area.

Philippine Tarsier

Tarsius syrichta

Range of *Tarsius syrichta*

Red Howler

Alouatta seniculus

Range of *Alouatta seniculus*

ROARING LIKE A LION. The howler, the largest monkey of the New World, has two outstanding characteristics: a formidable voice and a versatile tail. The angle of the lower jaw and the hyoid bone are unusually large, and the resulting howl produced by the males has been compared to the roar of lions and the roll of thunder. Their calls resound through the jungle day or night, audible for miles. Their other special feature is the tail: It is three feet long, as long as the monkey's head and body combined, prehensile, and naked on the underside toward the tip. Howlers hang freely by the tail, their feet dangling in the air; when they let go and fall, the tail will catch another limb in flight and check the drop. The tropical jungles of South America are the howler's range, extending from Mexico south to Ecuador, Bolivia, Brazil and Paraguay. There is a howler population also on the island of Trinidad. A 3-foot-long adult weighs about 20 pounds and has coarse hair of a deep reddish-brown color; other strains are yellowish-brownish or black, with individual variations. Led by one or two old males they live in troops of four to 30 individuals, each band occupying its own territory. Their diet includes leaves and nuts, roots and seeds, eggs and insects, small mammals and birds.

A VIVACIOUS ENTERTAINER. More than any other species of monkeys, capuchins delight children in zoological gardens, are sold in pet shops, perform in vaudeville acts, and beg for contributions, hat in hand, in those foreign countries where itinerant organ grinders still ply their trade. For they are smart and vivacious creatures, and natural-born actors. In the wild they are normally good-natured, chattering and screeching away, but occasionally have been observed to fly into a rage and bite a fellow member of the troop. Their range extends from Costa Rica in the north to Paraguay in the south, but it is not continuous. They live in the tropical forests of Brazil along the Atlantic, in Trinidad, and in Ecuador along the Pacific, but they do not occur in the northwestern part of the continent, nor in regions with an altitude of over 5,000 feet. As yet no satisfactory classification of the various species has been made; there are, however, two broad groups; one possesses hairy ridges on the sides of the head or horns of hair above the eyes; the coloration is grayish-brown. The other group does not have such adornments; in color it is black with white markings on chest, throat and face; also varying other color patterns occur. The partly prehensile tail is usually coiled.

Range of *Cebus capucinus*

White-faced Capuchin

Cebus capucinus

LIFE IN THE TREETOPS. These monkeys are ideally adapted to an arboreal life; their legs are unusually long, and while an adult's head and body may measure 25 inches, the prehensile tail will stretch over 35 inches. The latter is sensitive enough to pick up small objects and sturdy enough to serve as a useful fifth leg. The spider monkeys run rapidly over the branches, the tail forming an arch over the back; they hang by one hand or foot, jump to other trees 30 feet distant, and hardly ever descend to the ground. They don't like observers and sometimes throw dead branches at them. The four species dwell on a range that extends from southern Mexico to the Mato Grosso of Brazil and the central highlands of Bolivia. Their coloration is variable, grayish or brownish; some have flesh-colored faces but most forms have black faces with white rings around the eyes. They live in bands of 15 to 25 individuals, are active by day and feed on nuts and fruits. Their calls have been described as resembling the bark of a small dog or the whinny of a horse. They make entertaining pets and are also used in medical studies.

Red Spider Monkey

Ateles geoffroyi

Range of *Ateles geoffroyi*

Range of
Lagothrix lagotricha

Woolly Monkey

Lagothrix lagotricha

GENTLE FOREST DWELLER WITH A SAD MAN'S FACE. Rather deliberate, slow-moving and non-aggressive, the woolly monkey looks into the world with large, brown, "soulful" eyes. Of all monkeys it makes the most docile and tractable pet but misses its freedom and in captivity does not survive for long unless it is especially well cared for. If a person gives good care and treats it lovingly, it will become almost pathetically attached to its benefactor. The head-and-body length of an adult individual is approximately 27 inches, with a tail of 28½ inches and a weight of about 3 pounds. Its thick woolly fur looks as if it is cropped, with grayish, brownish or blackish upper parts; the color of the head is frequently darker than that of the body. The underparts have somewhat lighter tones, and the face is nearly black. The prehensile tail has a naked pad on its underside toward the tip; the short fingers are equipped with pointed nails. The range of the three species extends through Colombia, Ecuador, Peru and the upper Amazon valley of Brazil. The woolly fur, supplemented by a thick underfur, makes a warm coat and these monkeys also frequent cooler areas with altitudes of up to 7,000 feet. Active by day, they roam through the upper layers of the jungle in bands of about 12 individuals, frequently in the company of capuchins and howlers. More often than the other arboreal monkeys they descend to the ground where they stand upright, bracing themselves on the tail, and walk on their hind legs while keeping balance with their arms. They feed on fruits, flowers, and leaves but accept a variety of foods in captivity. Their varied calls seem to represent a wide vocabulary which includes a shrill scream of rage. The single young is born after a gestation period of four and one-half to five months; the baby woolly monkey clings to its mother's belly or rides on her back.

Range of *Leontideus rosalia*

Lion-headed Marmoset

Leontideus rosalia

A BRILLIANT BRAZILIAN. In the forests of eastern Brazil, particularly in the region of the Paraíba-Paraná river systems, one of the most colorful and exotic animals of the New World flits from branch to branch in small groups. A mane grows on head and shoulders and explains the name "lion-headed." The body is covered with long and silky hair of a striking metallic-golden or yellow color; its slender, narrow hands have elongated palms. The third and fourth finger are connected by skin, near the base. The largest adults of the species attain a head-and-body length of 15½ inches, with a weight of approximately 1½ pounds, but many individuals are considerably smaller. Uttering high-pitched sounds they leap through the trees in search of food which consists of fruits and nuts, insects and lizards, eggs and small birds. Tree hollows and crannies serve as shelters. They have a close family life, the father taking a real interest in his offspring which consists of one or two young; they are born after a gestation period of 134 days. He lets them ride on his back — a chore in which he takes turns with his mate — carries them to their mother at feeding time, prepares solid food for them after they have been weaned, by squeezing it between his fingers, and solicitously cares for them even after they have become fully grown, in approximately one year. Their life-span is estimated at 15 years. Two other species, closely related to the golden marmoset, are black with golden markings.

Cotton-head Marmoset

Saguinus oedipus

Range of
Saguinus oedipus

THE MONKEY WITH THE LONGEST TAIL. The pinché, or cotton-head marmoset, is another striking member of the marmoset group. Its crest of pure white fur extends toward the back as a mane; when the animal is angry the head plumes are said to stand erect like a headdress of ostrich feathers. The lower parts are white or gray, the upper parts and the exceedingly long, bushy tail are dark; the sides are often brown with red markings. The face is thinly haired and the large ears are naked; an adult has a head-and-body length of up to 1 foot, with a weight of 2 pounds. The range of the genus extends through southern Peru, northern Bolivia and southern Brazil; there these monkeys live in deep forests and open woods, hunting for insects and spiders, eggs and small vertebrates but also feeding on vegetable material. They proceed in small groups with rapid, jerky movements and communicate with high-pitched squeaks, including some flute-like calls and trills that sound like bird songs. Some groups redouble their vocal efforts when human beings are present. After a gestation period of five months one or two young are born; the father takes hold of the helpless babies and washes them, carries them to their mother at feeding time, at regular intervals of two to three hours, and calls for them again half an hour later. The young cling to his or their mother's body; they reach adulthood in 15 months. They breed in zoological gardens but have a high mortality rate.

Rhesus Monkey

Macaca mulatta

EUROPE

ASIA

Range of
Macaca mulatta

SACRED AND USEFUL. The rhesus monkey, one of the group called macaques, is sacred in his native range of India, notably in Bengal, and therefore is protected and treated with reverence by the religiously devout Hindus. To western man it is extremely useful; in thousands of specimens it is employed in biological and medical research laboratories, and in rhesus monkeys the Rh blood factor was first discovered and demonstrated. This species has been thoroughly studied and explored, and dozens of monographs have been written about it. Its physiology and psychology have become so well known that rhesus monkeys were selected as the first creatures to be shot, experimentally, into the stratosphere, thus preceding man in space flight. They easily adapt themselves to captivity in zoological gardens and can be taught various tricks for circus and variety acts. When they are young they make nice pets; when growing old, they become aggressive and bad-tempered; in captivity they will live for thirty and more years. They may grow to a head-and-body length of a little over 2 feet, with a tail half that long; a large male may weigh 28 pounds; their fur coat is yellowish-brown. In their range they live on a great variety of terrain, from forests to cultivated areas, from plains to mountains. They like to wander about in troops which may include as many as two dozen. Active during the day, they are equally at home in trees as on the ground, and are good swimmers. Their diet includes a great variety of animal food and plant material. They do not have a special breeding season; their one or two young are helpless and almost hairless when born and are nursed for a year; they begin to mate in four years.

ON THE ROCK OF GIBRALTAR. The barbary ape, a member of the tribe of macaques, is the only monkey encountered wild in Europe; its range on that continent is tiny, consisting only of "the Rock," and its total population is a troop of approximately 30 individuals. But larger numbers exist in North Africa in Morocco and Algeria, the old Barbary Coast which gave its name to the species. How the barbary ape crossed the Strait of Gibraltar is not known but it may have been taken there by Arab traders and warriors during the conquest of Spain. Here it is a cliff dweller but in North Africa it lives in almost any kind of terrain. According to a popular superstition, Gibraltar will stay under British rule as long as the barbary apes remain there. The folk tale is widely believed and the British garrison in Gibraltar sees to it that the apes are protected and do not go hungry. Consequently they have become half-domesticated and mischievous and sometimes treat tourists quite roughly. They are strong and courageous, and in defense of themselves or their young may even kill a dog. Occasionally two males quarrel viciously over a female. Their measurements are similar to those of other macaques, the head and body of a male reaching a length of about 2 feet and a weight of 28 pounds. The fur is rather shaggy and yellowish-brownish; their food consists of both animal and plant material. One or two young are born in a litter, at no particular season, and are nursed for a year.

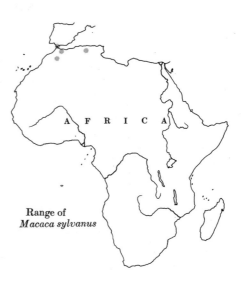

Range of
Macaca sylvanus

Barbary Ape

Macaca sylvanus

Pig-tailed Macaque

Macaca nemestrina

Range of *Macaca nemestrina*

IN THE TREES, ON THE GROUND, IN THE WATER. The pig-tailed macaque is largely arboreal but it is also active and agile on the ground and swims with ease. Its name refers to its semi-naked tail which is about eight inches long and curls up like that of a pig. An adult individual has an approximate head-and-body length of 20 inches; its face is naked, the coloration of its fur is yellowish-brown above and lighter below. Its range extends throughout India, southeastern Asia, and the principal islands of Indonesia. The dense tropical jungle is its habitat; there it lives in bands of about two dozen per unit, probably representing groups of harems. It is active by day, feeding on fruits, seeds and insects. One almost hairless young is born at any time of the year and nurses for about 12 months; twins occur rarely. The young mature in approximately four years. One closely related member of the genus which recently has played an important part in biological studies is the crab-eating or Philippine macaque. It has been widely employed in the research which led to the discovery of polio vaccine. This sturdy macaque lives in the mangrove swamps of river estuaries along the seacoast; it is a skillful swimmer and feeds on crabs, shellfish, and plant material.

THE EYELID MONKEY. The four species of mangabeys have an unusual facial feature; their eyelids are white and are visible at a considerable distance. Observations seem to indicate (though not conclusively) that these monkeys exchange signals by blinking their white eyelids. In equatorial Africa the genus inhabits a belt which from Guinea, Sierra Leone and Liberia curves southeastward into Uganda and Kenya. Mangabeys have also been reported in Angola on the Atlantic coast. These large monkeys grow to a head-and-body length of 35 inches, with a weight of up to 13 pounds. The tapering tail, approximately two and one-half feet long, is semi-prehensile; it can be wound around a branch and serves to support the body.

Normally it is carried straight up or bent toward the head; its tip is lighter in color than the lower part. Other characteristic features are much-used cheek pouches and webs between the fingers. In small herds of 4 to 12 individuals these monkeys forage mostly in trees, preferably in secondary forests, eating leaves and shoots, fruits, and occasionally some animal matter. The red-crowned mangabey pictured here has on its head a chestnut-red patch of hair; sometimes, however, the patch is blackish-brown or a mixture of olive and black; the single hairs have black tips. The fur is gray or brown above and grayish below. A strong beard adorns both cheeks. On the whole little is known about the life and the habits of these dwellers.

Range of
Cercocebus torquatus

Red-crowned Mangabey

Cercocebus torquatus

A SOCIABLE WANDERER. In troops of 50 or more the Chacma baboons roam over the savannas of eastern and southern Africa, led by big males who are aggressive and courageous. With the help of a few others they usually are able to ward off the baboons' worst enemy, the leopard. Physically baboons are well adapted to a terrestrial life, walk on all fours with a swaggering gait and run quite rapidly. With what has been called "a rocking-horse gallop" they attain a speed of up to 20 miles per hour. In certain regions they do a good deal of damage to plantations; occasionally they kill lambs for the milk in their stomachs, rip the upholstery out of parked automobiles, and in a few cases have attacked people. In South Africa's national parks they like to jump on the hoods of passing cars and enjoy the ride. An adult male may grow to a head-and-body length of 3½ feet, with a weight of 90 pounds. A dog-like protruding muzzle and naked buttock pads are characteristic features. The coat consists of coarse brownish and yellowish fur, with long hair growing around the neck and shoulders of males. The Chacma baboons are omnivorous, feeding on leaves and roots, fruits and seeds, eggs and young birds, grasshoppers and termites, grubs and scorpions. They are active by day and spend the night in rocky crevices, caves, or on large acacia trees. When grazing they keep up what sounds like a mumbling and grunting conversation but they also utter a loud bark. Constantly they groom each other and are unusually clean animals. The single young is born at no particular time of the year; at first it holds onto its mother's breast; later on it clings to her back.

Chacma Baboon

Chaeropithecus ursinus

Range of
Chaeropithecus ursinus

Hamadryas Baboon

Comopithecus hamadryas

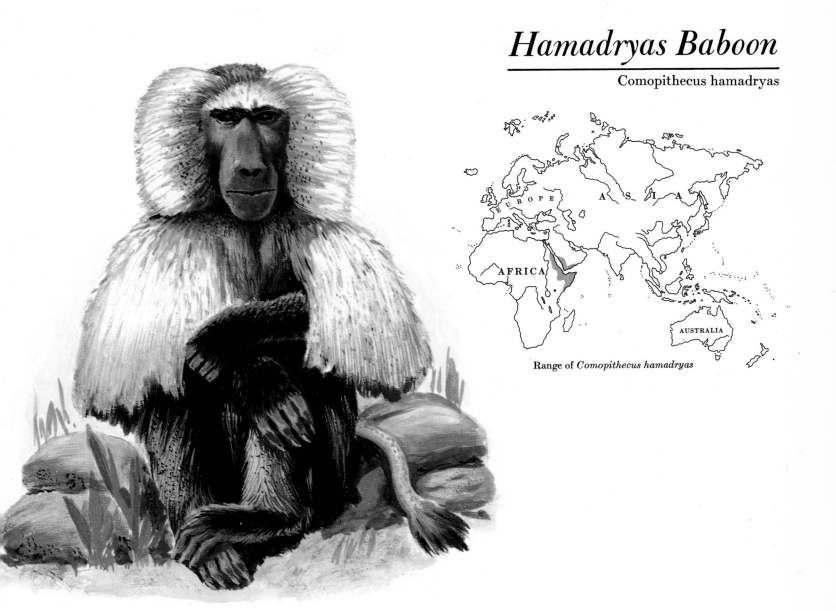

Range of *Comopithecus hamadryas*

THE SACRED MONKEY OF EGYPT. In ancient Egyptian temples and on monuments the hamadryas baboon is pictured as the helper and representative of Thoth, god of letters and in charge of the gods' writings. This monkey was worshiped as sacred and after its death was mummified and entombed. But in spite of this hallowed status the Egyptians put the hamadryas baboons to practical use, tamed them and trained them to climb trees and pick fruits for their owners. Today these monkeys are free in the wild, and roam the rocky plains and hills of Egypt and Ethiopia, Sudan and Somaliland; the range also extends into southern Arabia. An adult individual will attain a head-and-body length of 2½ feet, with a weight of 40 pounds. The brown fur of the young animals gradually changes to gray with advancing age; a sign of mature age in males is a heavy mane on neck and shoulders.

Their communities of 50 to 100 baboons live by definite rules under male leadership. Before the natives acquired firearms the baboons used to be a pest in certain regions; troops of as many as 300 would invade the grainfields and, ignoring the stones thrown at them, would drive the harvesters away. They travel on the ground and use rocky sites to look out for their enemies; but when a leopard catches a baboon, the other members of the troop only scream at the attacker and do not try to rescue the victim. Being omnivorous, they live on vegetable matter, small animals and insects. They drink daily, usually at noon. Their principal mating season occurs in May, June and July, but they also breed during the other months of the year. As a rule one young is born after a gestation period of six months; the occurrence of twins among the hamadryas baboons is rare.

Range of
Mandrillus sphinx

Mandrill

Mandrillus sphinx

A GROTESQUE PRIMATE. In equatorial West Africa, in Gabon, the central Congo and the southern Cameroon the grotesquely colored mandrill wanders about the forested areas in troops of about 50 individuals, especially in secondary woodlands where the food supply is plentiful. The general appearance of these animals is monstrous; all the males have ridges and grooves on each side of the nasal bone, the skin of the grooves being purple and that of the ridges blue. The nasal bone which extends to the muzzle and the nostrils stands out in a brilliant vermillion. The buttock pads shine in lilac hues with edges of reddish-purple. Females and the young lack the brilliant purple color in their facial grooves, and their noses are black. A male adult, with crest, mane and beard, may attain a head-and-body length of 2½ feet and weigh about 120 pounds; its fur has tawny-greenish tones above and yellowish hues below. In the wild mandrills are greatly respected as formidable foes, ready to fight and to use their strong teeth; when excited and angry their colors shine even more brightly. Although they shelter and sleep in trees, they spend most of their time on the ground, looking for fruits, nuts, and other vegetable material and turning over stones and debris in search of insects and small animals. In captivity they live up to 40 years.

Guenon

Cercopithecus aethiops

A HOST OF RELATIVES. The guenons which live in Africa south of a line from Gambia on the Atlantic to Ethiopia include approximately 12 species, but the number of existing forms is legion. Anatomically all belong to the same genus, but in appearance they offer a wide variety of colors and adornments. They may or may not have, or combine, such features as long white whiskers; variously colored whiskers; faces with partly blue or violet skin; a tuft of hair on the chin; a bunch of yellow hair on the cheek; a white, blue or red nasal spot; greenish-gray or brown upper parts; blackish or red bellies; single hairs encircled in various colors; whitish strips on the thighs. The largest members of the genus have a head-and-body length of 27½ inches and a weight of about 15 pounds; the tail, up to 34½ inches long, is prehensile in the young. When enraged these monkeys show their teeth and confront the adversary with a savage grimace; this habit has been responsible for the name guenon which means "fright" in French. In troops of six to 30 they roam the woods and forage on leaves and fruits, grass and roots; some forms drink water regularly, others receive sufficient liquids from their vegetable food. The single young holds on to the underfur of its mother, its tail interwined with hers.

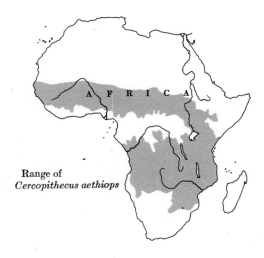

Range of
Cercopithecus aethiops

Indian Langur

Presbytis entellus

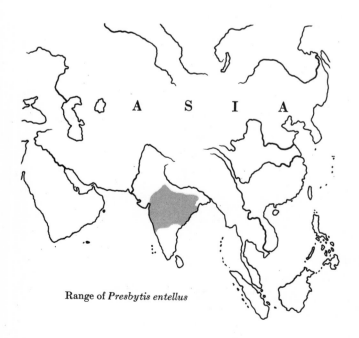

Range of *Presbytis entellus*

THE LEAF-EATERS. The langurs or leaf-eating monkeys have an unusually diversified habitat. Some can be observed in Hindu villages at sea level, cavorting around temples or on roads, while others are encountered in the snow-covered evergreen forests of the Himalaya, at an elevation of 13,000 feet. There seems to be an upward migration in the spring and a downward migration in the fall. The range of the 14 species of langurs extends from Indonesia westward through Indochina, southern China, and India to Ceylon. The largest specimens have a head-and-body length of 2½ feet, with a weight of 40 pounds, but many forms are smaller. All, however, have certain characteristic features. The tail is extremely long, measuring up to three and one-half feet; the well developed hands are also unusually long; the eyes are shaded by a row of black, bristle-like hairs, and the hair on the crown is arranged radially in some forms and as a crest in others. The fur is grayish-brownish-blackish, somewhat lighter below. Several forms have light-colored markings, and various mutations occur. These monkeys are active by day, feeding on leaves and seeds, flowers, fruits and perhaps some small animals; for the night they retire into the treetops. Pictured here is the hanuman, sacred or common Indian langur.

THE LONG-NOSED MONKEY. The outstanding feature of this species, referred to in the popular name "proboscis" and in the name of the genus *Nasalis,* is the protruding nose which in older males hangs over the face like a pendulum. The female nose is less conspicuous, and that of the young is turned up. The purpose of this facial growth is unknown, and the habits of these quiet and gentle animals have hardly been explored. They form a single species and are found in the delta areas and river-banks, the nipa palm groves and mangrove swamps of Borneo. They are arboreal and feed on leaves, fruits and other vegetable matter. The head-and-body length of an adult male is about 2½ feet, with a weight of 50 pounds; the females are considerably smaller, and approximately half that weight. Their fur is chestnut to cinnamon-brown with grayish-creamy underparts. In small groups they are active by day; the call of the male has been described as a long-drawn-out and nasal honking; the softer cry of the female has been compared to that of the goose. Attempts to keep these monkeys in European and American zoological gardens have largely failed; the imported specimens did not thrive in captivity and died soon after their arrival.

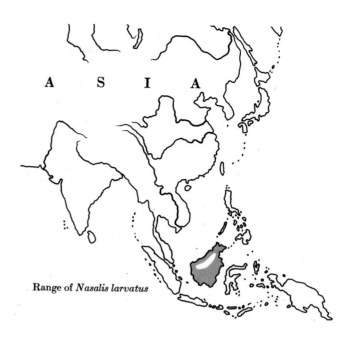

Range of *Nasalis larvatus*

Proboscis Monkey

Nasalis larvatus

Black and White Colobus Monkey

Colobus polykomos

Range of
Colobus polykomos

MONKEY FUR FOR WARRIORS' SHIELDS. Floating down the Blue Nile, a wildlife watcher will find the black and white colobus monkeys an exciting sight. In troops of about 20 they cavort in the tall trees ashore, some of them parachuting from high to low branches while their cape of long hair acts to soften the fall. Their hair and their spectacular coloration — a jet black background fur, a white frame around nose and eyes, a white cape, and patches of white on the tail — made the colobus a marketable object. African warriors used its pelt and hair to adorn their shields and exporters sold it to furriers and milliners in Europe and America. This species is sometimes called the "guereza" but in Africa it is generally called "colobus." At present the colobus is protected by law but some natives still hunt and eat it. Besides the variety described above there are others of the same species without white markings or with different hair arrangements. The range of the colobus is extensive, from Ethiopia to Senegal and the Cameroon in the west and to Tanzania and Angola in the east and south. Dense forests are its preferred environment; in the mountain ranges it is encountered at heights of up to 10,000 feet. It spends practically its entire life in trees feeding on leaves and buds. A big male may weigh 27 pounds, with a head-and-body length of 2 feet 3 inches and a tail almost 3 feet long. It has either no thumb or only a tiny spike. When excited it barks loudly. Besides the colobus species described here two others exist; one is the black-and-red colobus, the other has a fur of olive tones.

THE TREE WALKER. That is the translation of *Hylobates*, the name of the genus to which all gibbons belong. They are indeed the champion-acrobats in the world of mammals, swinging from branch to branch, trapeze-fashion. The hoolock gibbon pictured here occurs in a variety of fur colors, from black to brown to gray and cream; many of the newly born young are almost white; it takes them a few years to acquire their final color shade. The hoolocks, like all gibbons, have a strong whooping voice which can be heard over considerable distances. Their mixed vegetable-animal diet consists of fruits and leaves and also of eggs, birds and other small creatures. Assam, Burma and western Yunnan in China circumscribe the range of the species.

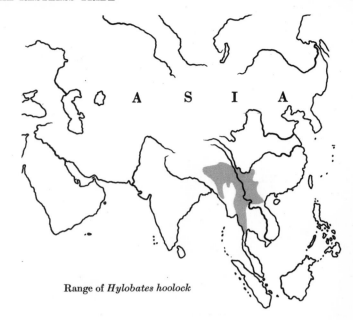

Range of *Hylobates hoolock*

Hoolock Gibbon

Hylobates hoolock

Range of *Hylobates lar*

White-handed Gibbon

Hylobates lar

THE SWINGING WALK. These clean, gentle and intelligent primates, considered to be the most agile of all mammals, use their forelimbs rather than their hindlimbs for locomotion. Hanging by their arms and employing their hands as hooks they swing, trapeze-fashion, from branch to branch. Sometimes their long swings become leaps covering 30 feet or more. When balancing on a large branch or proceeding on the ground they normally walk upright and keep their equilibrium by raising their arms high. The six species of gibbons cover a wide, tropical range from Assam in India eastward to Sumatra, Java and Borneo, including Burma, Thailand, and Indochina. They inhabit rain forests at various elevations, from sea level to heights of 8,000 feet. An adult male gibbon may attain a head-and-body length of 25 inches, with a weight of 17½ pounds; the tail is missing. The coloration of the gibbons is highly individualistic, with hues ranging from creamy white to brown to almost black. The species pictured here has white hands and feet, and a white fringe surrounding the face. Many gibbons are born white, then gradually change and arrive at their definite coloration when they are two, three or four years old. Largely tree-dwellers, gibbons feed on leaves and buds, fruits and eggs, young birds and insects. Small family groups of two to six individuals live on their own territory and defend it against intruders. They are monogamous and closely attached to each other. For safety, two or three huddle together while sleeping, sitting upright in a treetop. Their whooping calls, audible over long distances, are said to represent a considerable vocabulary of definite meanings.

INTELLIGENT INTROVERT. In contrast to the extrovert chimpanzees, the orangutans of Sumatra and Borneo are rather placid and shy, but numerous stories attest to their reasoning powers; toward human beings they show considerable interest. In captivity they are often sick and are not suitable as pets, for their strength is tremendous and they become extremely dangerous when aroused. A characteristic habit of theirs is the building of sleeping platforms of branches and vines in trees. Whether they use these "beds" repeatedly or build new ones every night is not certain. Large leaves are used as blankets in rainy weather. An adult male has an approximate length of 5 feet, an arm spread of 7 feet but no tail, and a weight of about 165 pounds. The shaggy coat is dark- or reddish-brown. Orangutans travel by swinging from branches. On the ground they walk on all fours.

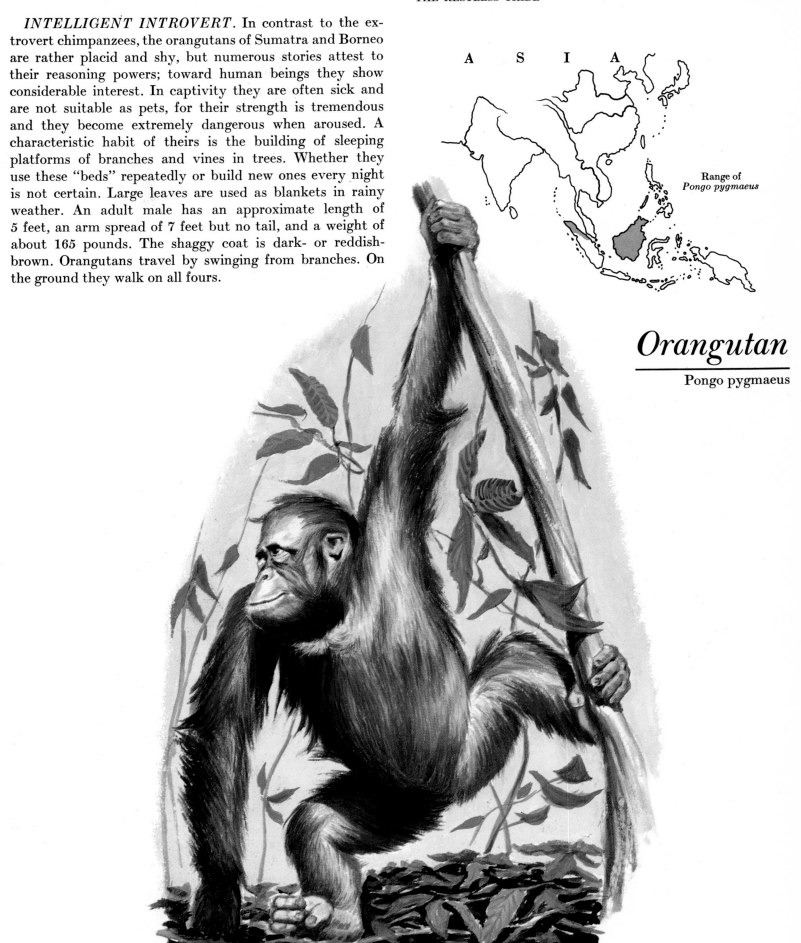

A S I A

Range of
Pongo pygmaeus

Orangutan

Pongo pygmaeus

Range of
Pan troglodytes

Chimpanzee

Pan troglodytes

IS THIS THE MOST INTELLIGENT ANIMAL? The answer is probably yes. It is known to work out simple problems by reasoning; it can use uncomplicated tools; it "speaks" a "language" of 32 different sounds which have a significant meaning; and it recognizes most colors. Its multiplicity of facial expressions rivals that of humans. This inquisitive, excitable primate lives in the rain forests of tropical Africa where it feeds on vegetable material but also kills various animals and eats their meat. When standing upright, a grown-up male may measure 5½ feet in height he may weigh 175 pounds while the females are smaller. The fur is black and so is the bare face; nose and ears as well as hands and feet have a pinkish flesh color. Chimpanzees troop through the jungle in groups of up to 20, led by a male. They walk with an erect posture or on all fours, the body bent forward. The shelter they build for the night is abandoned the next morning. A single young, rarely twins, is cared for by its mother for two years; breeding begins at the age of 12 years, and a healthy specimen may live for 40 years.

THE MOST POWERFUL PRIMATE. The popular picture of a huge male gorilla furiously beating his chest and charging a native is wrong; the gorilla does not have this habit, is shy and retiring, and does not attack anyone without reason. If irritated, however, it growls and roars and is dangerous because of its innate strength. This physical power makes the gorilla also unmanageable as a pet; it may act well behaved until in periods of anger it drops all restraints normal to human beings. In this sense the behavioral sciences have found the gorilla an interesting subject of research. Of the two varieties of gorilla the lowland type is encountered in the jungles of the Congo River valley and the mountain type on the ranges in and around Albert National Park, at elevations up to 12,000 feet. An adult male may stand upright at a height of 6 feet, with a weight of about 610 pounds; its outstretched arms will measure 6½ feet between fingertips. Its coarse fur is black and may become gray on the back with advancing age. If it is a mountain gorilla it will carry a top knot of long hair on its head. Toward evening each troop constructs sleeping platforms, one at the base of a tree for the male leader, and the others high up for the females and young. Apparently they build new shelters every day. They are vegetarians and feed on plant material.

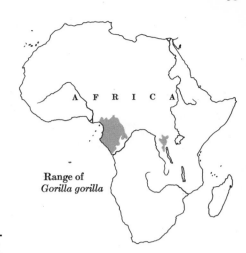

Range of
Gorilla gorilla

Gorilla

Gorilla gorilla

Dental Deficients

ANTEATERS, SLOTHS AND ARMADILLOS — EDENTATA

The word *Edentata* means "without teeth," a strange name for an order in which the majority of members do possess teeth; one of them, the giant armadillo, has in fact one hundred teeth, more than almost any other mammal. As a partial justification it should be mentioned that the anteaters are lacking teeth completely and that the others, while possessing teeth, are without incisors and canines. Tree sloths and armadillos have non-enameled cheek teeth which grow continually as long as the animals live. The order, consisting of three living families and 14 genera with just over 30 species, is strictly a New World dweller; in the United States it inhabits sections of the south central and southeastern states; from there the range broadens southward into Mexico, Central and South America. The smallest member of the order is Burmeister's armadillo, with a head-and-body length of less than 6 inches, and the largest is the giant armadillo which attains a length of 3 feet and a weight of 120 pounds. The habits of the various *Edentata* vary greatly; the armadillos and the giant anteater are terrestrial and diurnal or nocturnal; two other anteaters, collared and least, usually live in trees and are nocturnal; the sloths are strictly tree dwellers and feed at night. All of them occur singly or in pairs; sometimes, however, small bands of armadillos are encountered. Anteaters feed on termites and ants, sloths are vegetarians, and armadillos eat insects and small animals, plant material and carrion. In captivity the members of the order have lived from 12 to 16 years.

PANGOLINS — PHOLIDOTA

The word *Pholidota* means "scaled animals." This order consists of a single family and genus whose seven species live in the African and Asian tropics. Overlapping scales cover the upper parts of their tapering bodies; they enable the pangolin to curl into a tight spiral in case of danger; if a female nurses a young, she hugs it within the ball of her body. A more active weapon is an obnoxious liquid which the pangolin ejects from a gland of the anal region and which is well aimed at the attacker. For shelter the terrestrial pangolins excavate holes several feet deep which end in a roomy circular chamber; or they occupy the abandoned burrows of other animals; the arboreal species retire to hollow trees. Local folktales describe the pangolin's "ant bath;" it sits down in an ants' colony, raises the scales and lets the ants creep under the scales, whereupon the scales are lowered and the ants crushed. The pangolin then wades into a river or lake, opens the scales and lets the dead ants rise to the surface. Scientists do not dismiss the story; the animal may use this method to have the ants clean its skin under the scales.

Giant Anteater

Myrmecophaga tridactyla

GROTESQUE BUT EFFECTIVE. This big anteater looks antediluvian, clumsy and tiny-brained, but it is well-equipped for its specialized life. The three large and one small claws on each hand — the animal walks on its knuckles to protect its long nails — are most powerful and rip open logs, anthills and termite nests. Then its tongue shoots out of its cylindrical snout into the opened galleries and is soon covered with cocoons, eggs and ants. The tongue is worm-like, up to two feet long, but has a diameter of only one-half to three-quarters inches; salivary glands coat it with a sticky, gummy saliva to which the insects adhere. The earth that is swallowed on this occasion aids in the process of digestion. The giant anteater does not dig a burrow or establish a permanent home but wanders about until tired. Then it curls up at any protected spot and covers head and body with its plumelike tail. The range of the single species extends from British Honduras in Central America south to the Argentine Chaco. Savannas and swampy forests are its preferred habitat. The head-and-body length of an adult male is approximately 4 feet, with a weight of 50 pounds. The color of its coarse and stiff coat is gray, with a white-bordered black stripe running diagonally over its body.

Range of
Myrmecophaga tridactyla

Range of
Choloepus hoffmanni

Two-toed Sloth

Choloepus hoffmanni

A LIFE SPENT UPSIDE DOWN. The sloth performs all functions of life while hanging on its claws from a branch. In that position it "walks," eats leaves and fruit, sleeps with its head resting between its forelegs, mates and delivers the young. It turns right side up only when it descends into a lake and swims with a kind of breast stroke. This animal looks like an integral part of a tree branch, especially when it forms a hanging basket by placing its claws together. The mimicry effect is heightened by a greenish hue which spreads over its fur; for tiny pits in its hair are filled with green algal growth and adapt the body to the background of leaves and mosses. The species pictured here has a range from Nicaragua to central Brazil and Peru. An adult specimen will reach a length of somewhat over 2 feet and a weight of about 20 pounds. The grayish-brown fur consists of dense underfur and an outer coat of long hair. The claws — two on each front leg and three on each hind leg — are formidable hooks. Its movements are slow but it can defend itself valiantly; strikes with its claws and its bites inflict ghastly wounds.

A DIGGER WITH A HUNDRED TEETH. This is more than twice the number of teeth usually grown by mammals; gradually it loses them, however, with advancing age. More formidable tools are its front claws; the one on the third finger measures up to 8 inches. These claws are used for digging a shelter and also for getting food out of the ground: termites and other harmful insects, worms and snakes, and also carrion. By doing so the armadillo performs a useful task and should not be hunted and killed. Its range is the eastern part of South America where it usually lives near rivers. Adults reach a head-and-body length of 3 feet 3½ inches and a weight of 133 pounds. The coloration is brown but a whitish band runs around the lower part of the shell; its 14 to 17 bands give a rigid, armor-plated appearance but the bands are movable and the animal is quite agile. Its usual form of locomotion is walking on its hind legs with the tail as balance while the front feet almost touch the ground. The armadillo is inoffensive and will run away from an enemy or will curl up; since it cannot completely close its shield around its body, in the form of an inaccessible ball, the latter method is not often effective. One or two tough-skinned young are born.

Range of
Priodontes giganteus

Giant Armadillo

Priodontes giganteus

Range of *Tolypeutes matacus*

IT ROLLS ITSELF INTO A PERFECT BALL. Its three movable bands — occasionally two or four — separate two large shields whose lower insides are free of skin and provide room for head, tail, and legs whenever the armadillo decides to close the trap and form a sphere. Of the approximately 20 species of the family the two species of three-banded armadillos are the only ones which can do this. They are the rarely seen *Tolypeutes tricinctus* which inhabits northeastern Brazil toward the center of the country, and the more common *Tolypeutes matacus* whose range reaches from Bolivia through the wilderness of Brazil's Mato Grosso to the Gran Chaco of Paraguay and the pampas of Argentina. The Latin Americans have various popular names for this curious native, for instance *mataco* (referring to Mato, the wilderness), *tatú bola* (alluding to the "ball") and *apara*. The official Spanish name *armadillo* is related to the English word armor. The ball is an effective defense, but not always. If a major predator happens along, for instance an adult jaguar, the attacker can wedge the sphere between its jaws and crack and crush shell and contents. The head-and-body length of this armadillo is up to 17 inches, its color blackish brown; like most of its relatives it usually walks on its hind legs, barely touching the ground with its front feet and using the short tail for balance. Ants and termites are its principal food, dug with powerful claws from the soil or from under the bark of trees.

Three-banded Armadillo

Tolypeutes matacus

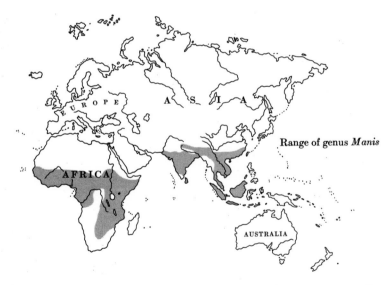

Range of genus *Manis*

Giant Pangolin

Manis gigantea

THE MAMMAL THAT LOOKS LIKE A LIZARD. So unique are the pangolins' features that science has created a special order for them. This order is composed of but a single family and a single genus. There are, however, seven species, four in tropical Africa south of the Sahara and three in the general area of India, Indonesia, and Southeast Asia. The two extraordinary features of this mammal are its scales and its tongue. The horny overlapping scales cover the back, the top of the head and the limbs; they grow out of the thick skin and range in color from yellowish to dark brown. Their function is to protect and defend; in a crisis the pangolin curls up in a spiral in such a way that the soft parts of its body are covered and inaccessible — it is nearly impossible to unwind the spiral; the sharp edges of the scales stand erect, and since the

scales are movable they twitch. Would-be attackers are usually afraid to tackle the dangerous-looking creature and trot off. The other incredible feature consists of a tongue so long that it has to be kept in a special muscular sheath which runs from the mouth through the chest to the pelvis. With its strong front claws the pangolin rips open the mounds of ants and termites, which are the animal's favorite food, shoots out its tongue into the exposed galleries and licks up large numbers of insects which adhere to the sticky saliva. It is unafraid of the swarms of attacking termites; it closes tight its ears and nostrils, clamps down its thick eyelids, and gets rid of all others by a vigorous shaking. The head-and-body length of the largest males is approximately 2 feet ten inches, with an equally long tail; they reach a weight of 60 pounds.

The Gnawers

PIKAS, RABBITS AND HARES — LAGOMORPHA

The order *Lagomorpha* includes two families, the pikas forming one and the rabbits and hares the other. The geographic range of the order comprises all the landmasses of the earth except Antarctica and some islands; it has been introduced to New Zealand and Australia where it has become a pest. Its smallest member has a head-and-body length of 5 inches, the largest of 2½ feet; the weight ranges from 3½ ounces to 10 pounds. The incisor teeth of these animals grow throughout life, i.e., the part worn off by gnawing is replaced by new growth from the root. The pikas, also called conies or whistling hares, resemble small rabbits; they are active by day and live in colonies, usually in rocky areas. They store grass near their burrows and seem to converse in a high-pitched whistle. Among the rabbits and hares the large majority of species do not live in colonies; those that are poor runners excavate burrows as family shelters; the fast runners merely build grass nests or "forms" for their offspring. All feed on grass and herbaceous vegetation but eat the bark of young trees in emergencies. All *Lagomorpha* have a unique system of getting double value from their food. Their excrement consists of dry pellets which are left on the ground, and moist pellets which are picked up and swallowed; in this way the food travels through the digestive tract a second time.

RODENTS — RODENTIA

Rodentia is the largest of all orders; it includes more than half of all living species of mammals, and while it is impossible to determine how many billions of rodents inhabit the earth, their total number far exceeds that of all other animals combined. The 32 families and more than 350 genera occupy practically all land areas of the globe; any environment suits them, from jungle to tundra, from desert to modern megalopolis. They lead an underground life or spend their days in trees, on the ground or in the water; they leap and run, climb and glide, swim and dive. Beneficially they keep down many insect pests but destructively ruin field crops and food stores. Some of them — beaver, chinchilla and muskrat — produce beautiful and costly furs; others — guinea pigs and hamsters, rats and mice — are indispensible in biological research. Some like the rats carry parasites which transmit deadly diseases, including the bubonic plague. Man conducts a continuous war against the more destructive rodents; but being resourceful and having a high birth rate they survive. The incisor teeth of all rodents grow at the base throughout the life of the animal; the edges of the teeth are worn down by gnawing food; besides, the rodents frequently grind their teeth on available hard surfaces to aid in the process. The surface of the teeth is harder on the outside than on the inside; this has a chisel-like, self-sharpening effect.

HAY-MAKER. All of the 14 species of the genus *Ochotona* have the curious custom of making hay; they live in regions of severe winters and do not hibernate; therefore they have to store food for the cold months. During the summer they collect weeds, grasses and all kinds of plants; they even climb low trees and venture out on the limbs to cut twigs. What is not eaten on the spot is dragged to flat rocks, spread out in the sun and cured as hay. These accumulations of dry plant materials, often exceeding a bushel in volume, are constantly moved out of the rain or to a sunnier curing place. Finally they are stored; the rock-dwelling pikas keep their hay on dry spots under overhanging rocks; the plains-dwelling pikas stack it near their burrows. The harvesting grounds are in communal use but the pika of the American West considers its burrow, its hay-pile and the ground around it to be its own territory and loudly warns potential intruders. Another characteristic feature of the pikas is their habit of whistling; their high-pitched calls can be heard all day and sometimes at night; this has resulted in such popular names as "whistling hare" and "piping hare." A sharp bark is also uttered. The head-and-body length of an average specimen is 8 inches, with a weight of 4½ ounces. The soft, dense coat is grayish-brown with lighter colors below. Two or three times a year litters of two to six young are born. The pikas form a family with a single genus; 12 species range in Asia, from Siberia to the Himalaya, one inhabits Alaska and the Yukon and the species pictured here lives in the Rocky Mountains and Great Basin areas of Utah, New Mexico and California.

Range of
Ochotona princeps

American Pika

Ochotona princeps

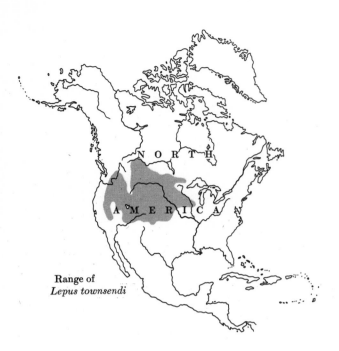

Range of
Lepus townsendi

NOT A RABBIT BUT A HARE. The 26 species of hares — distinguished from the rabbits by their huge ears and large hind feet — have an almost worldwide range now. In North America they occur as far south as Mexico, are rare in the East but a landmark in the West where several species are known as jack rabbits. In long leaps they run through the thin vegetation of prairies and plains, sit up or fight each other at mating time; two males will box with their forefeet or kick with their hind feet, also maul their female partners. Otherwise they are timid, relying on a speedy escape. "Coursing jack rabbits" with fast dogs was a popular pastime in pioneer days. Adult specimens will attain a length of 27½ inches and a weight of up to 15½ pounds. Their grayish-brown fur is used in the manufacture of felt. They do not dig burrows but hide their one to seven (normally three or four) young at various spots in dense vegetation where the mother visits and nurses them. While young rabbits are naked, young hares are well furred and have their eyes open.

White-tailed Jack Rabbit

Lepus townsendi

Old World Rabbit

Oryctolagus cuniculus

A COUSIN OF THE COTTONTAIL. While the European or Old World rabbit resembles the American cottontail, its way of life is quite different. It digs interconnected "rabbit warrens" which may be inhabited by as many as 150 gregarious specimens. There every pair produces six litters a year, each consisting of three to nine naked and blind young. Abortion is so frequent that only 40 percent of the litters conceived are actually born. This species may grow to a length of 17¾ inches, with a weight of 4¾ pounds. In its fur black and light brown hairs are mixed; its eyes are big, its claws long and straight. Its food consists of herbs, grasses, and other plants. A native of southwestern Europe and northwestern Africa, it has been introduced to many other parts of the world and has become a serious pest in Australia where natural enemies are lacking. Spreading of a contagious virus disease has helped to control the rabbit population. From the European rabbit the numerous strains of domesticated rabbits have been derived and selectively bred as producers of meat or fur, as laboratory animals, or as pets in beautiful colors.

Original range of *Oryctolagus cuniculus*

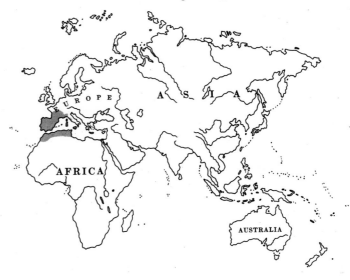

Eastern Gray Squirrel

Sciurus carolinensis

Range of
Sciurus carolinensis

PLANTER OF TREES. Squirrels all over the world bury acorns, conifer seeds, hickory nuts, walnuts and other nuts in the ground as a reserve for lean days. Many of these stores are forgotten and turn into trees. There are 55 species of squirrels in most of Europe, Asia and the Americas from southern Canada to northern Argentina, and all are similar in anatomy and habits. They love nuts, and because of a special construction of their lower incisors can open one in a matter of seconds; but they also eat fruits and buds, insects and birds' eggs. The gray squirrel attains a length of up to a foot, with a weight of 2½ pounds. Its winter shelter is in a hollow tree, its various summer nests are in the forks of tree branches. Two litters of one to five, normally two or three young are born each year. Equally well known is the smaller red squirrel with a brownish-red fur coat and white underparts. It is a vociferous forest dweller which scolds approaching persons or animals with clucks and whistles, grunts and chatterings.

A WELL-ORGANIZED TOWN DWELLER. The prairie dogs which inhabit America's prairies and plateaus from North Dakota to northern Mexico maintain a fascinating social organization. Each one of their towns which may have hundreds of inhabitants is divided into wards, in accordance with the lay of the land, and each ward into families which consist of a male, one to four females, and the young of the past two years, two to three to a litter; quarrels and disputes are settled in a hierarchic order, the adult male having the last word. The burrow may be as deep as 16 feet; on its two or three side tunnels grass nests are constructed. On top the soil from the burrow is heaped as a volcano-like cone to keep out the rain water. At the holes the prairie dogs like to sit upright and look out; seemingly they converse in a chirruping chatter; these little barks are responsible for the animal's name although it is a kind of squirrel. Several different alarm calls are distinguishable, one against an enemy on the ground, one against a foe from the sky, one for help and one an all-clear signal. An adult prairie dog may grow to a length of not quite 1 foot and weigh about 3 pounds; its fur is yellow-gray on the back and lighter underneath. Grasses and herbs are its food. There are five existing species.

Range of
Cynomys ludovicianus

Prairie "Dog"

Cynomys ludovicianus

Eastern American Chipmunk

Tamias striatus

Range of
Tamias striatus

HANDSOME HOARDER. Chipmunks spend their days busily stuffing their expandable cheek pouches with seeds and fruits, flowers and buds, mushrooms and bulbs; sometimes they eat insects and birds' eggs. Seeds and other dry foods are carried to underground burrows and stored for winter use. When the cold season arrives the chipmunks retire to their shelters where they remain in a torpid condition; during warm spells they awaken and feed on their stores. Of the two genera the genus *Eutamias* inhabits a large section of western North America from Canada's Northwest Territories to northern Mexico. In the Old World the genus is represented from Siberia to northern China. The habitat varies from pine woods, redwood groves and mountainous brushlands to plains and temperate rain forests. The genus includes 17 species of which the largest attains a head-and-body length of 6½ inches, with a weight of 4½ ounces. The most characteristic feature of the chipmunk's coat is the handsome design of five black or blackish-brown stripes with four white stripes between them. Otherwise the upper parts are yellowish, the lower ones white. Two to eight young are born in the spring. Similar to the western American and Asiatic species but somewhat larger is the genus *Tamias* of southeastern Canada and the eastern United States. When fed, these rodents become pleasant pets.

ENGINEER OF THE ANIMAL WORLD. As is well-known, beavers build dams, lodges, canals and ponds with unceasing industry and great accuracy. They do so in order to secure their food supply of bark and roots, twigs and leaves, and to maintain a safe winter shelter. The dams consist of mud and stones, poles and sticks; some of them are as long as 2,000 feet and create ponds of considerable acreage. The lodges are built of the same materials to a height of up to six feet; several underwater entrances lead to a sleeping chamber above the water level. A number of beaver houses form a colony whose members collaborate peacefully; by gnawing at the base they fell trees of a diameter of up to two feet, preferably willows or aspens, poplars or alders. They cut the trunk into suitable pieces and drag them to the water or dig a canal to the site and float the logs to their final destination. The range of the American beaver extends from Alaska and Canada to the Rio Grande. The European beaver is restricted today to a few colonies in France, Germany, Poland, the Soviet Union and Scandinavia. The largest beavers grow to a length of 4 feet and a weight of 70 pounds but most of them are smaller. Their thick undercoat is protected by a long outer coat, deep brown or yellowish-brown in color, with black feet and tail. The latter is broad and horizontally flat, scaled and naked.

Range of
Castor canadensis

American Beaver

Castor canadensis

Range of *Dicrostonyx groenlandicus*
Range of genus *Dicrostonyx*

Greenland Lemming

Dicrostonyx groenlandicus

DO LEMMINGS COMMIT SUICIDE? **The folk tale that in years of famine thousands of lemmings plunge into the sea and drown is quite true; but they do not commit intentional suicide. The story of these small rodents begins with the fact that they reproduce rapidly; they feed on plant material which in their Arctic environment is soon depleted while new vegetation grows slowly. In cycles of three to four years the overpopulation of lemmings forces thousands to seek new feeding grounds, and a strange phenomenon occurs. They emigrate in a straight direction, regardless of obstacles; when they come to a river or lake they swim across and continue their journey from the other bank. Some groups reach the ocean and plunge into the water intending to reach the other shore; they swim until they are exhausted and drown. Other thousands are killed by predatory animals or starve to death. This occurs quite regularly with the true lemmings (genus *Lemmus*) of which the Norway lemming is best known. The collared or Arctic lemmings (genus *Dicrostonyx*) usually undertake only shorter treks. Lemmings inhabit the Arctic regions of North America and Eurasia.**

Range of *Mesocricetus auratus*

Golden Hamster
Mesocricetus auratus

The Scandinavian peninsula and northwestern Russia are the range of the Norway lemming. The genus *Dicrostonyx* attains a length of 5¾ inches; its grayish-reddish coat turns pure white during the winter; Eskimo children have coats trimmed with it. The genus *Lemmus* is about half an inch shorter and keeps its grayish-brownish coat summer and winter. Three to nine young are born, after a gestation period of three weeks. Pictured here is the species known as the Greenland lemming.

HOARDER AND PET. Golden hamsters are natural hoarders; they possess huge cheek pouches which extend to the back of their shoulders, and when they stuff them with leaves, seeds, fruits and bits of meat they double the width of their heads. Their range extends from the Balkans in Europe to Asia Minor, the Caucasus, the Levant, and northwestern Iran; steppes and brushlands are their habitat. There they live alone in burrows they have

excavated and fight intruders of their own kind; sometimes they feed by day but usually are more active at night. Adults attain a head-and-body length of up to 7 inches, with a weight of 4½ ounces; the females are somewhat larger than the males. The fur is reddish-brown, with an ash-colored stripe across the breast; the females have 14 to 16 nipples and every month produce litters of six to seven young (more in captivity) which in turn start breeding when they are approximately two months old. Their life span is estimated at two to three years. In the early 1930's it was discovered that hamsters of Syrian stock made amusing pets since they are easily tamed, clean, free of disease and without body odor. Domesticated strains were developed in Europe and reached America in 1938. Now they are found in thousands of homes as children's pets, and in zoological gardens and biological research laboratories. New colors have been created which include albino, cream and harlequin.

SUPERBLY EQUIPPED FOR AQUATIC LIFE. The muskrat, an expert swimmer and diver, can stay under water for twelve minutes, in salt or freshwater marshes, in lakes or rivers. Its hind feet are partially webbed and have a "swimming fringe" of close, stiff hairs, and its tail is laterally flattened so that it can be used as a rudder. In an open swamp it constructs a house of plant material worked into growing reeds, a dome-shaped mound as high as three feet with a diameter of up to six feet. Communication with the outside world is by tunnel and underwater exit. In a river it digs a burrow in the bank above the water mark, with tunnels leading into deep, non-freezing water. It also builds slides for land-to-water communication and for play. Its range can be circumscribed by a line from Labrador south to South Carolina, Texas, Arizona and Baja California, north to Alaska and east to Labrador. It has a head-and-body length of up to 1 foot 1 inch, with a weight of 4 pounds. On a soft, dense underfur a coat of long guard hairs looks handsome with silvery brown to black shades. This coat is in great demand and the primary source of trapped fur on the market; the pelts are abundant and reported to be 40% more durable than other furs. The muskrat feeds mostly on water plants and occasional fish and mussels. Its meat, served as "marsh rabbit," is tasty. Several annual litters produce one to eleven, usually five to seven young. The name muskrat refers to the animal's musky odor. Introduced to Europe, it has become a pest there, tunneling dykes and irrigation dams.

Range of
Ondatra zibethicus

Muskrat

Ondatra zibethicus

Range of *Rattus norvegicus*

OUR WORST VERMIN. In the world of mammals the genus *Rattus* is the largest, with 570 recognized forms; it occurs in practically every part of the earth. Its most prominent representatives are the black and the brown or Norway rat. The black species, a native of Asia Minor and the Orient, migrated to Europe during the Crusades and to America on the ships of explorers. The albino strain used in research has been derived from the black rat. The brown rat, native to eastern Asia, appeared in Europe in the middle of the 16th century and in North America during the Revolutionary War. The brown rat, with a weight of up to 17 ounces, somewhat larger than the black species, is the one which has settled in the neighborhood of man. Both forms are smart, curious and adaptable, omnivorous, and a pest of the worst kind. They cause tremendous food spoilage, infest sewers and warehouses and do a worldwide annual damage amounting to billions of dollars. Besides, they carry the hosts of bubonic plague, typhus, rabies, a type of food poisoning and several other diseases. It has been estimated that during the last thousand years the epidemics transmitted by rats have killed more human beings than all wars combined.

Norway Rat

Rattus norvegicus

House Mouse

Mus musculus

Range of *Mus musculus*

PET AND PEST. This delicate, pretty and clean little animal does some good: It cleans up table crumbs and keeps down cockroaches and other vermin. Its domesticated white strains make delightful pets for children and are extensively used in laboratory research. On the other hand it does a great deal of damage causing food spoilage and carrying the hosts of typhus, spotted fever and perhaps other epidemics. It is so prolific that at times it becomes a plague. The Central Valley of California, for instance, was overrun by exploding mouse population twice in this century. The house mouse is a native of the Old World but on ships has spread to every continent; today it is as well adapted to Antarctic camps as to desert huts. Some forms remain always in the wild, subsisting on plants; the house dwellers eat every existing human food plus soap, glue, and similar substances. Some forms move from houses to fields in spring and return in the fall. The head-and-body length usually does not exceed 4 inches, with a weight of 1 ounce. The fur is brown or black above, whitish below. Breeding goes on all year long, the three to 12 (normally four to seven) young are born in a nest of soft material; there may be as many as five litters per year, and the new generation begins to mate at an age of 35 days.

NO ATTACK BUT A DEADLY DEFENSE. The slow-moving, phlegmatic porcupine never attacks anything but it defends itself most effectively. It erects its quills, turns its rear toward the aggressor, and swings its tail at the enemy. The sharp, barbed quills detach themselves from the porcupine as soon as they touch the skin of the attacking animal. According to folklore the quills are shot or thrown, but that is not true. Normally they cannot be removed from the adversary's face or paw except with human help; so they work their way inward, penetrate an inner organ or cause gangrene and death. The range of the North American species extends from Alaska and Canada through the United States to northern Mexico; excepted are our southeastern states. It prefers to live in forests of evergreens and poplars. With a head-and-body length of up to 2 feet 10 inches, the average weight is 15½ pounds although a large specimen may weigh 40 pounds. The upper parts of the body have a woolly underfur in which long and stiff guard hairs grow; among the latter the quills are lightly attached to the skin. The all-over color is brown or blackish; the quills are whitish at the base. The porcupine is largely nocturnal and does not hibernate. During the summer it feeds on leaves and twigs, during the winter on evergreen needles and bark, often causing the death of the denuded trees. Its excessive liking of salt turns it into a pest near camps; it will chew anything that contains salt or retains salt from human perspiration, including ax handles, saddles, and paddles. The single young is well developed and climbs trees at the age of two days.

Range of *Erethizon dorsatum*

North American Porcupine

Erethizon dorsatum

Guinea Pig

Cavia porcellus

Range of *Cavia porcellus*

NEITHER A PIG NOR FROM GUINEA. The other languages are as deficient as English in naming this little gnawer. In Spanish the guinea pig is called *conejo de las Indias,* "rabbit of the Indies;" in Portuguese *porquinho da India,* "little pig of India;" in German *Meerschweinchen,* "small sea pig." In fact this animal is a rodent of about 20 species living in South America, from Colombia and Venezuela south to northern Argentina. It occurs in almost any kind of terrain, from swamps and savannas to the borders of forests and rocky areas. In those regions it has been domesticated since time immemorial and besides the llama was the only domestic animal of the Incas; they liked its meat which has a fine texture and an excellent taste. The head-and-body length is up to 14 inches, with a weight of a little over 1½ pounds. In the wild form the fur is long and quite coarse and of grayish or brownish color; in the domesticated form it is shorter and smoother, and the colors are white or black, brown, red, or yellow, or they are mixed in various designs. In the wild the cavies, as they are also called, live in groups of five to ten in their own burrows or in the abandoned holes of other animals; they leave them at dusk and on their runways through the dense underground run to the various stands of plants which are their food. They are extremely shy and flee when disturbed. Since they are gentle and do not bite, they are kept today as children's pets and also have proved valuable as research animals in the fields of nutrition and heredity, serology and medicine in general. They mate throughout the year and have litters of one to four, more in the tame form. The wild species from which the domesticated type has been derived is *Cavia porcellus.*

A FUR SO FINE YOU CANNOT FEEL IT WHEN YOU TOUCH IT WITH YOUR FINGERTIPS. It seems that at one time chinchillas lived at lower altitudes but were decimated by carnivorous predators so that they gradually moved to the high Andes Mountains. There they established themselves above the treeline at heights from 9,800 to 19,600 feet and grew their warm, silky coats as a protection against the climate, a development which almost led to their extinction. For when it became known that Europe paid fantastic prices for chinchilla pelts, ruthless trapping resulted. Hundreds of thousands of pelts were exported until Chile, Bolivia and Peru enacted protective laws; now the population is on the increase again. Chinchilla farms are operating in various parts of the world but while the days of a hundred thousand dollar price for a chinchilla coat are past, the fur is still the costliest of all. It is not only silky, soft and extremely dense but also has a sophisticated color, pearl, bluish- or brownish-gray; the underparts are whitish-yellowish; the long whiskers are black and white. An adult specimen may attain a head-and-body length of 15 inches, with a weight of 2¼ pounds. On their barren mountains they live in colonies and feed on any plants available at that altitude; they hold their food in their hands and sit on their haunches while eating. Their environment offers hardly any water but some Andean plants store dew and they contain sufficient moisture for the chinchillas. The species mates for life; litters of one to six are born one to three times a year. The young run about a few hours after birth and may live for ten years in the wild; some captured specimens have reached the age of twenty.

Range of *Chinchilla laniger*

SOUTH AMERICA

Chinchilla

Chinchilla laniger

Waterbound Hunters

WHALES, DOLPHINS AND PORPOISES — CETACEA

These mammals, which live in a completely aquatic environment, are divided into two living suborders, the *Odontoceti* which have teeth and a non-symmetrical skull, and the *Mysticeti* which are equipped with membrane-like baleen plates and have symmetrical skulls. The former feed on fish and such ocean fauna as squids and octopi (only the killer whale devours other animals also), and the latter on plankton, a mixture of tiny sea animals. The order consists of eight families, about 38 genera and more than 90 species and inhabits all the seas of the world, as well as a few rivers and lakes. Its smallest member has a length of 4 feet and a weight of 50 pounds, and the largest a length of 100 feet and a weight of up to 150 tons. This enormous size is attained because their bodies float in water and do not have to be supported. While the tail flukes of fish are attached vertically, those of the aquatic mammals are set horizontally. The limbs of the latter have developed into flippers which are covered with skin. There are no hind limbs, and none are needed since the cetaceans propel themselves by moving the tail up and down; the fins help to balance and steer the body. What keeps them warm in cold water is the blubber, a fibrous mass saturated with fat and oil, a layer just below the skin. There are no external ears but the sense of hearing is sharp, as is that of touch; their vision is limited, and they are unable to smell. When diving, the blowholes (one in the toothed whales, two in the baleen whales) are closed; the tear glands secrete an oily substance which shields the eyes from irritating saltwater; and the heartbeat is decreased. Spongy bones and oil-filled cavities are helpful in the floating process.

The fountains blown into the air, a spectacle often enjoyed by ocean travelers, are not water spouts but consist of water vapor exhaled from the lungs. Various sounds produced by cetaceans have been recorded; it is assumed that they represent inter-individual communication but also are used for echolocation as a means of determining place and direction and of locating food supplies. The single young is born in the water after a gestation period of 11 to 16 months, and is pushed to the surface for air; it nurses, however, under water, and its growth is rapid; the milk is rich in calcium and phosphorus. Since time immemorial cetaceans have been hunted for meat and oil, spermaceti and blubber, bone and baleen. The killings were greatly increased when in 1864 the harpoon gun with a delayed explosive head was invented and when in the late 1930's big factory ships began to operate, independent of harbors. Since 1937 whales have been protected by international regulations.

"MOBY DICK." The sperm whale has not only won literary fame but has deeply influenced America's economic history. The 800 whaling ships that sailed from New Bedford, Nantucket and many other ports hunted mostly sperm whales, and sperm whale oil lighted the lamps of the young United States and of much of Europe. The world's oceans are the range of this whale; gregariously and polygamously it lives in schools of up to 20 individuals, forming schools of hundreds for the annual migration to tropical waters during the winter and to temperate waters for the summer. The head-and-body length of a male may reach 60 feet while that of the female rarely exceeds 40 feet. The coloration is dark-bluish to black, paler with increasing age. Its most striking feature is its enormous head which accounts for one-third of the whale's overall length. Half of the head is a huge tank, the spongy tissue which contains a light, fine wax, the raw material for the famous spermaceti candles; today it is used for oiling precision instruments. On the underside of the head a disproportionally thin jaw is equipped with up to 30 peg-like conical teeth on each side. In order to reach its principal food supply of squid, octopus and cuttlefish these whales dive to depths of 1,200 feet and sometimes re-emerge with wounds and scars of combat with a giant squid. Occasionally they vomit a substance called ambergris; it is gray, aromatic and highly prized by the perfume industry.

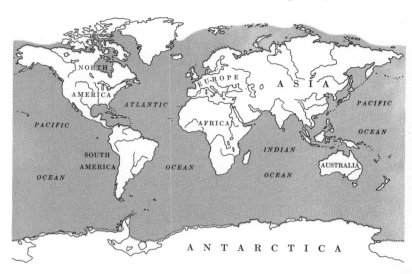

Range of *Physeter catodon*

Sperm Whale

Physeter catodon

A MOST INTELLIGENT OCEAN DWELLER. Dolphins are the star performers at oceanographic exhibits on both our Atlantic and Pacific coasts, catching fish thrown high into the air, leaping through burning rings and showing similar skills. They are said to help a wounded companion by pushing him up to get air, and reportedly can be trained as undersea messengers. The most common species of eastern North America is the bottle-nosed dolphin, shown here, whose three-inch beak resembles the top of an old-fashioned bottle. This species has a worldwide range but prefers bay and inlet waters not deeper than 60 feet. It grows to a length of 11½ feet and a weight of 440 pounds; the upper side is black, bluish-black or gray, the lower side is lighter. Swimming in schools of five or more it feeds on any fish available including sharks, also on shrimps and squids. The calf is about three feet long at birth and weighs up to 26 pounds. The species whose leap-and-dive antics entertain passengers of ocean ships is the common dolphin which also has a worldwide distribution; this brown or black species with a white belly is smaller but faster than its bottle-nosed relative, with a length of up to 8 feet and a weight of up to 166 pounds. Its top speed is said to be as high as 25 knots; the other dolphin species of the genus is considerably slower.

Bottle-nosed Dolphin

Tursiops truncatus

Range of *Tursiops truncatus*

Killer Whale

Orcinus orca

THE OCEAN'S MOST VORACIOUS PIRATE. A pack of killer whales — there may be as many as fifty swimming in close formation — spreads panic wherever it appears. With a mouth big enough to swallow a young walrus and with up to 28 huge, razor-sharp teeth in each jaw, the killer whales sometimes attack a prey far larger than themselves. Several of them will take on a baleen whale, for instance; they tear it to pieces, rip out its tongue and bite off its lower jaw. Or one of them will dive and from below crush a three-foot-thick ice sheet; sea birds and seals resting there slide into the water and the killer's mouth. In the stomach of one average 20-foot male 14 seals and 13 porpoises were found. This vicious glutton inhabits all oceans but is most frequently encountered in the Arctic and Antarctic seas; its tolerance for temperature changes is unusual. Its appearance is striking: black above and white below, with white patches above the eyes. A highly maneuverable swimmer, it proceeds at an approximate rate of 8 mph; its huge dorsal fin sticks out of the water when the whale stays near the surface, acting as a stabilizer. Its occasional long leaps are a remarkable habit; it jumps over a distance of 45 feet.

Range of *Orcinus orca*

Range of *Megaptera novaeangliae*

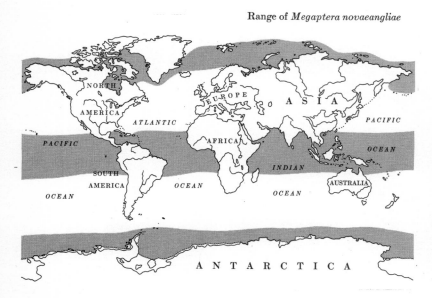

Humpback Whale

Megaptera novaeangliae

EQUATORIAL MEETING. During the summer the northern stock of the humpback whale lives in the icy waters of the Arctic in small mixed groups. The southern stock inhabits the waters of the Antarctic during that season in large, separate communities which keep to themselves. When winter approaches the northern races migrate south and the southern ones go north, both traveling as far as the Equator where they meet. On this occasion they may mingle, but whether they do is not certainly known. Often they are encountered in coastal areas. They used to be very common along the shores of California, Australia and New Zealand before they were overhunted. An adult male humpback may attain a length of about 50 feet, with an average weight of 32 tons. Its coloration is rather striking, the throat and breast being white and the back black. The body is stocky and curved, humpback fashion; head and flippers are covered with irregular outgrowths, and barnacles, seaweed, worms and other parasites frequently plague this whale. It feeds on fish and crustaceans, mostly a planktonic shrimp. Male and female mate while lying side by side; they "caress" each other with loud, heavy, alternate blows of their flippers, and while frolicking sometimes jump clear out of the water. The gestation period is one year; the young is about 13 feet long at birth.

Blue Whale

Sibbaldus musculus

*THE BIGGEST ANIMAL ALIVE AND THE LARG-
EST THAT EVER LIVED.* With a length of 70 to 100
feet and a weight of up to 124 tons the blue whale surpasses in size even the dinosaurs and other monsters that
inhabited the earth at an earlier stage. A single specimen
will yield between 70 and 80 barrels of oil; therefore it used
to be hunted extensively. The color of this whale is dark
slate-blue, and up to 100 grooves cover the underside.
Usually a film of yellowish microscopic algae covers its
lower surface and accounts for its second name, "sulphur-
bottom whale." Its food consists mostly of krill, tiny
shrimp-like crustaceans half an inch to an inch in length.
When it takes a deep dive it may stay under water up to 20
minutes; this is followed by several minor dives of 12 to
15 seconds each. When expelling its breath it "spouts" and
blows a column of vapor-laden air high into the atmo-
sphere. Passing travelers have the illusion of a fountain
rising in mid-ocean. During the summer it dwells not far
from the Arctic and Antarctic icepacks but during the
winter, swimming at a speed of 10 to 12 knots, it migrates
to subtropical waters. There it lives singly or in small
groups and breeds with two-year intervals between preg-
nancies. The single young is 25 feet long at birth; on rare
occasions twins are born.

Range of *Sibbaldus musculus*

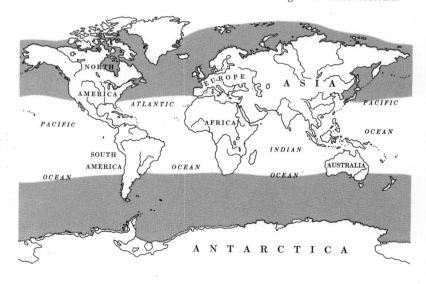

Predators

TERRESTRIAL ·FLESH-EATERS — CARNIVORA

The globe is inhabited by seven families and about 100 genera of terrestrial flesh-eaters; they are absent only from the Antarctic and some islands. Their smallest member is the least weasel, 7 inches long and weighing 2½ ounces; the largest is the brown bear of Alaska which attains a head-and-body length of 10 feet and a weight of 1,730 pounds. All carnivores have claws which in the case of the cats (with the exception of the cheetah) can be retracted. Some members, like the bears, walk on soles and heels; others, like the cats and dogs, proceed on their toes. Most of them are good climbers and all are able to swim. The polar bear is semi-aquatic and the sea otter actually lives in the water, but all others are terrestrial. Their way of life is predatory; they hunt mostly by scent, stalk their prey or pounce on it, kill it and eat the fresh meat. Lions and leopards are especially fond of the intestines of their prey; they disembowel their catch and eat the vitamin-holding viscera and intestines first, then feed on the red meat. Raccoons and bears are omnivorous, with a mixed meat-and-plant diet; hyenas are scavengers, and jackals thrive on carrion. One or two litters a year are the rule; one to 13 young are born, which are covered with fur but blind and helpless.

AQUATIC FLESH-EATERS — PINNIPEDIA

The aquatic flesh-eaters are closely related to the *Carnivora* and have sometimes been treated as a suborder. The seacoasts of the world are their range, with the addition of a few rivers and lakes. With the exception of the tropical monk seal they inhabit polar and temperate waters. The name *Pinnipedia* means "feather-footed," and refers to their flattened fore and hind flippers. In the water they propel themselves with their limbs, each of which has five webbed digits. When submerged, their external ears and nostrils are closed, and their eyes are protectively cushioned in fat. A thick layer of blubber directly under the skin helps to provide warmth and buoyancy. Pinnipeds breed on small, isolated islands or rugged coasts; they mate once a year and give birth on land. The single young is able to swim at birth and develops rapidly; it is nurtured by its mother's rich milk which contains 50 percent fat. Smallest member of the order is the ringed seal with a length of 4 feet and a weight of 200 pounds, largest the elephant seal, 22 feet long and weighing 4 tons. Various pinnipeds are hunted for their fur, oil and meat. When the fur is prepared for the market, only the dense growth of the soft, short underfur is retained while the coarse, long guard hairs are removed.

THE ONLY FLESH-EATING NON-MARSUPIAL IN AUSTRALIA. When European explorers discovered the Australian continent, they found there, in considerable numbers, a wild dog which they considered a native animal. However, naturalists soon recognized that this dog was entirely different from Australia's original fauna which consists of marsupials. Therefore it was generally supposed that the dingo was not a native of the country and that it was introduced by aboriginal immigrants in early prehistoric times, a supposition still in question because of the discovery of their remains in Pleistocene deposits. This sleek, wolf-like dog with large pointed ears, a bushy tail and a yellowish-brown to blackish coat of dense hair, occasionally with white markings, is about 2½ feet long and 2 feet tall. It has the reputation of being bold and fierce, cunning and crafty. At one time after the country became settled, the dingo was almost exterminated by sheep ranchers and poultry farmers because of its depredations of livestock; but it made a comeback when rabbits were introduced to Australia, multiplied rapidly, and furnished a steady and easily available supply of food. Hunting alone, in pairs or in small packs the dingos also kill kangaroos and other game. Adult specimens cannot be domesticated but the Australian aborigines search for puppies, take them home, tame them and train them as hunting dogs to locate opossums, lizards, snakes and the like. In a wild state dingos yelp and howl but do not bark; however, if domesticated and living near dogs, they bark by imitation.

Dingo

Canis dingo

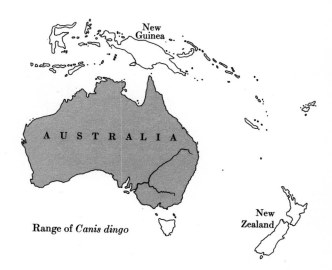

Range of *Canis dingo*

Gray Wolf

Canis lupus

Range of *Canis lupus*

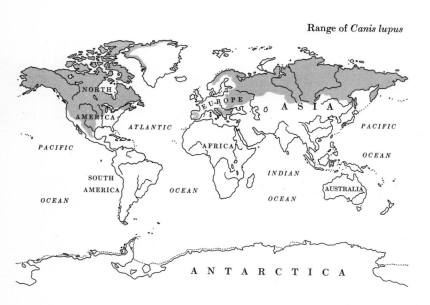

HOW DANGEROUS ARE WOLVES? Western literature, especially that of Germany and Russia, abounds with stories of packs of wolves viciously attacking travelers on horseback or in sleighs. While this may have happened in exceptionally severe winters of famine, the wolf in general is not nearly as bloodthirsty as it is reputed to be. It is adaptable, intelligent, loyal to its mate — they seem to stay together for life — and shy of human beings rather than aggressive. The gray wolf once lived in all of North America, Europe and Asia but has been driven out of nearly all inhabited areas; it survives mostly in the barren forests of the high north. There it hunts in packs of three to 24, killing deer, elk and moose. But it also eats mice and other small animals, fish and carrion. It grows to a length of up to 4 feet with a shoulder height of 3 feet 2 inches and a weight of 175 pounds. Its gray coat is mottled with black while the underparts are whitish-yellowish; the Arctic and Alaskan wolves are always white. Three to 13 young are born in a lair dug by their mother; they can expect to live up to 16 years.

VOICE OF THE PRAIRIE. The howling of a coyote far away, during a still, clear, starry night, has been poetically described as a voice of longing and loneliness. In American folklore this little wolf-dog has been associated largely with our Southwest but it is really an all-American animal now. While the gray or timber wolf has lost territory, the coyote has considerably extended its range which now reaches as far north as Alaska, as far south as Central America, and as far east as New York state. Its head and body measure up to 3 feet in length, with a weight of up to 28 pounds; its fur coat is brown mixed with gray and black. This adaptable and clever canine usually hunts alone, eating rabbits, rodents and carrion; occasionally it kills livestock, such as sheep and goats. There may be a relationship between the method of hunting and the hunter's speed. The wolf which does not run faster than 28 miles per hour, cooperates in packs; the coyote which attains a speed of 40 miles per hour, prefers to hunt singly. Occasionally strange hunting partnerships between coyotes and badgers have been observed. Coyotes apparently mate for life; the average litter consists of five to ten pups which are born in a cave, a hollow tree or a burrow. Whether the wolf and the coyote are ancestors of our domestic dogs remains an open question; both look almost exactly like some of our widely distributed domestic breeds, and it is probable that several races of dogs have at least a certain amount of wolf or coyote blood in their veins.

Range of
Canis latrans

Coyote

Canis latrans

Black-backed Jackal

Canis mesomelas

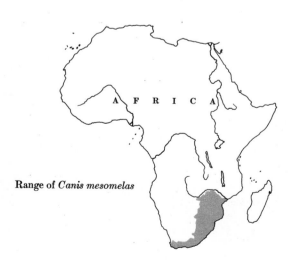

Range of *Canis mesomelas*

IN THE WAKE OF THE LION. Jackals like to follow lions and leopards, watch them at their meals and devour the scraps after the cats have left. This habit has brought about a human comparison; a persistent hanger-on is called a jackal. Of the three species the golden jackal has a dirty-yellow coat with red and black touches; its range extends from central Africa through the Middle East to Burma and Thailand. The side-striped jackal which wears a pair of light and dark stripes on each side is a native of eastern and southern Africa; and the black-backed jackal, which is pictured on this page, inhabits the same African territory. All of these jackals interbreed easily with domestic dogs. The head-and-body length of an adult specimen is approximately 2½ feet, with a weight of about 24 pounds. Jackals spend the day in deep woods or thickets of vegetation and hunt at night; they are good runners and in the open savannas achieve a speed of 35 miles per hour. If they are not looking for the lion's leftovers they run down young antelopes and other small animals; but they also eat insects and spiders, plant material and carrion. The black-backed jackal always hunts in pairs throughout the year, and when the two partners raise a family, their two to seven puppies go hunting together with them as soon as they are 6 to 8 weeks old. The eerie nocturnal yapping of the jackals is well-known on the plains.

A MOST INHOSPITABLE HOME. The Arctic fox inhabits places where few other mammals could survive. In 1951 a French expedition discovered a group of them living on the icecap in the center of Greenland at a height of 10,000 feet, with temperatures of 60° below zero. Arctic foxes have been observed to cross the strait between Baffin Island and Greenland on ice floes. On the other hand some wander south for 100 miles into the forest. They inhabit the Arctic regions of both the eastern and the western hemispheres and survive well; but they have to feed on whatever edibles come their way, dead or alive, lemmings and fish, young seals and whales washed ashore, or the leftovers of the polar bear's meals. Their burrows are natural deep-freeze compartments where they store dead birds and small mammals for the winter. An adult male may reach a head-and-body length of 26 inches, with a weight of 20 pounds. The fur is beautiful, the coloration depending on the color phase; specimens of the white phase are snow-white in winter and brown in summer. The foxes of the blue phase are dark grayish-bluish in summer and paler in winter. The blue foxes are very rare on the Canadian mainland but constitute about half the fox population in Greenland. White and "platinum" foxes are now raised on farms, either on small islands where they roam at will, or in enclosures where selective breeding is possible.

Range of *Alopex lagopus*

Arctic Fox

Alopex lagopus

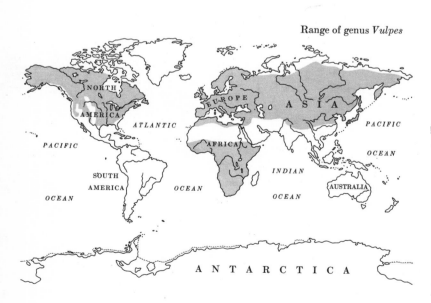

European Red Fox

Vulpes vulpes

Range of genus *Vulpes*

"FOXY" — ALERT AND KNOWING, SMART, CLEVER (WEBSTER'S NEW INTERNATIONAL DICTIONARY). The fox's formidable reputation is partly based on fiction; however, the fox is indeed a highly intelligent animal. Dogs instinctively hate foxes, and during hunts the fox seems to take delight in outsmarting its foes, obliterating its scent by wading along a brook, showing up in back of the hunting party, and trying other tricks. The chase is an exciting challenge, and at times the fox seems to display a sense of humor. Among its other clever acts is its method of getting rid of fleas; gradually it backs into water. Occasionally it may raid henhouses, but the damage is far outweighed by a beneficial habit; the extermination of rodents. Besides mice and other small animals, fruits and grasses, eggs and insects are on the fox's menu. The genus of red foxes includes seven species and has a tremendous range. It inhabits most of North America north of Mexico, Europe, most of Africa and Asia. Wooded areas and brushlands are its habitat. The adult male may attain a head-and-body length of 34 inches, with a weight of 20 pounds. Its pelt varies in color from yellowish-red to reddish-brown, with white or gray underparts. Red foxes appear to be monogamous; both parents take care of their four to ten young.

TOY FOX OF THE DESERT. This smallest of all foxes is one of the most handsome of all animals, with fluffy, soft, long fur, big dark eyes, and a heavily furred tail. Its baby-like appearance is enhanced by the whimpering calls it utters when disturbed. The color of its coat varies from reddish-cream to creamy-white. In the sandy environment of the desert this constitutes protective coloration designed to make detection by enemies difficult. The advantage of the mimicry, however, seems to be neutralized by the fennec's nocturnal habits. It does not emerge from its burrow until the dark of night has descended. The intention of nature is not quite clear here. The range of the fennec extends through the arid regions of North Africa, including the Sahara, and through the Sinai Peninsula and Arabia. An adult male has a head-and-body length of about 16 inches and may weigh 3 pounds. It is lively and agile; a specimen in captivity has jumped, from a standing position, two feet straight up into the air or four feet horizontally. In the wild it lives in burrows which it excavates at great speed; according to a native saying the fennec "sinks into the ground." Occasionally communal groups exist with connecting links between the burrows. The question may be asked how in a sterile environment the fennec obtains its food. The fact that in captivity fennecs forever rake and scratch the ground indicates that in their habitat they dig for their food, pulling small rodents and birds' eggs, lizards and locusts out of holes in the sand. They also eat plant material. Desert travelers sometimes see fennec tracks many miles from water holes; this seems to prove that the little foxes can live without liquids for considerable periods of time. However, when fennecs appear at an oasis they drink copiously. Two to five young are born in March or April; they have a life-span of 10 to 12 years.

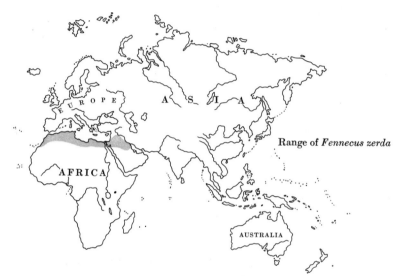

Range of *Fennecus zerda*

Fennec

Fennecus zerda

Eastern Gray Fox

Urocyon cinereoargenteus

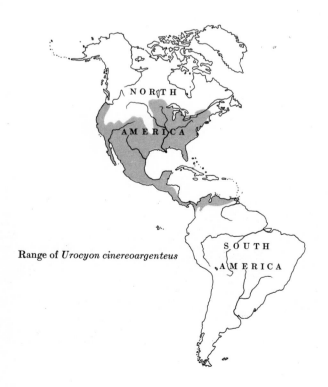

Range of *Urocyon cinereoargenteus*

"TREE FOX" OR "MOUNTAIN CAT." In some parts of the United States the gray fox is called "tree fox" because of the facility with which it climbs trees, an unusual trait in the family *Canidae*. It takes refuge in trees, chases squirrels up trees, and also climbs them for no apparent reason. Some Latin Americans call it *gato del monte,* or "mountain cat," because it is frequently encountered in rocky areas. Its range extends from southern Canada through the United States, Mexico and Central America to northern South America. It seems to be most common in the dry and rocky sections of our Southwest, in western Mexico, and the pine barrens of Venezuela. A different species is found on several islands near the California coast. The eastern variety has a length of up to 2 feet 3 inches and a weight of up to 15½ pounds. It is gray, with the exception of the white throat and underparts and the sides of the neck and the flanks which have a rusty shade. There is a market for its pelt, but since it is coarse it is not considered a quality fur. The animal's diet consists of animals, insects, and plants; it seems to be more of a vegetarian than the red fox and likes fruits and seeds. Two to seven young (normally three or four) are born in cavities and crevices; lately, lairs have been discovered even under farm buildings. When caught young, gray foxes make affectionate pets, far more so than red foxes.

A LITTLE KNOWN SAVANNA DWELLER. **Our** knowledge of the bush dog is scanty; in the wild it lives in regions far removed from civilization, and only a few zoological gardens possess living specimens. Before it was officially observed in a wild state, it was scientifically described from fossils discovered in Brazilian caves. Its range is the northern and eastern parts of South America, from Panama through eastern Colombia, the Guianas and Brazil to Paraguay, and also in eastern Peru and northern Bolivia. The bush dogs live in woodlands or on savannas, particularly on those of the huge Amazonian forest; they seem to like sandy terrain. They are reported to hunt in packs at night, running, swimming and diving well, even swimming under water. They have been observed to chase pacas into the water and to pursue them there. Small animals, mostly rodents, are their principal food. By day they rest, often sleeping in abandoned burrows of armadillos; but bush dog dens dug into a hillside have also been found. This stocky, round-eared, short-legged and short-tailed dog which has been compared to a fat and overlong dachshund has a head-and-body length of up to 2½ feet. A male may weigh as much as 15½ pounds. The color of its coarse fur is brown but changes from lighter to darker hues between head and tail; the front parts have a whitish or orange shade while the hind sections are darker, occasionally almost black. The few bush dogs kept in zoological gardens have adapted themselves well to captivity and in many ways behave like domesticated dogs. They have also a short bark like that of dogs. One of their habits is amusing: they seem to talk to themselves with whining, chirruping, squeaking and whistling, almost bird-like sounds. In the San Diego Zoo litters of four or five have been born; in the wild the numbers may be about the same.

Range of *Speothos venaticus*

Bush Dog

Speothos venaticus

A BOLD AND SILENT KILLER. There is something uncanny about a pack of 20 to 30 dholes gliding through the dusk in complete silence, running at moderate speed and tirelessly trailing their prey, every one knowing what to do, taking turns, finding short cuts and finally closing in on the catch. The operation is carried out by scent. Their boldness is astonishing; not even the tiger is safe from them; occasionally they may kill one but they respect him; he is the only game for which they break their silence with a special rallying call. They slaughter also bears and leopards but more regularly wild sheep, antelopes and deer, water buffaloes and gaurs, nilgais and bantengs. From time to time they move to a new territory. They do not attack human beings. Their Asiatic range is wide. It includes wooded and rocky areas in Siberia, China and Korea, India and Indochina, and Java and Sumatra. The dhole has a length of up to 3 feet and a weight of up to 46 pounds. In warmer regions it wears a yellowish-brown coat throughout the year; in cold territory its heavy coat, fortified by thick underfur, is brownish-grayish during the winter and brown during the summer. The dhole is often called a wild dog, particularly in India, but although it looks like a dog and in many ways behaves like a dog it does not belong to the same genus. It is untamable; it has long fur between its pads; and its dentures and skull are somewhat differently constructed; the female has 12 to 14 nipples as compared with 10 for the dog. The dhole cannot bark either although it can howl and uses a special mating call. The two to six young are born at all seasons.

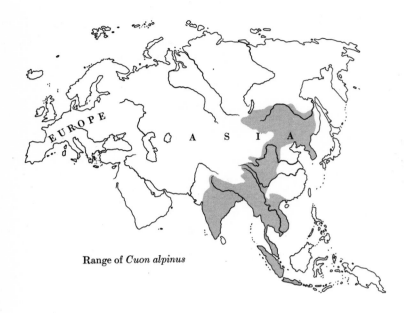

Range of *Cuon alpinus*

Dhole

Cuon alpinus

Cape Hunting Dog

Lycaon pictus

STRATEGY OF THE HUNTING PACK. These strange-looking animals whose range includes various parts of Africa south of the Sahara are perhaps the most systematic pack hunters of the animal world. Their method is that of flushing out and running down their prey, not by speed but by tireless perseverance, working in relays and cutting corners at strategic moments. Almost always they catch their victim and kill it in the most cruel fashion, snapping at it and tearing pieces of flesh from its body; when it collapses from loss of blood the dogs eat it alive; a pack of twelve will finish a good-sized game animal, perhaps an antelope, a sheep or a goat, in fifteen minutes. In packs of not less than six and not more than 60 they attack any animal they can overwhelm; they even tackle old, tired lions and kill and eat them but are usually frustrated by more vigorous specimens. They enjoy hunting and accompany the chase with a weird rallying call; they kill more than they can consume and are among the worst depredators of African wildlife. They are equally at home on the plains and on the East African mountains, as high up as the tree level. Although they do not attack man they are not afraid of human beings and sometimes take a threatening attitude. They are said to have a deep contempt for domesticated dogs and kill them on sight. The Cape hunting dog attains a length of up to 3½ feet, with a shoulder height of 2 feet and a weight of 51 pounds. Its coat shows black, orange-yellow and white patches in every conceivable design. The hair is so thin that here and there the blackish skin shines through the fur. It has only four toes on each foot and its body emanates a strong odor. Its six to eight young are born at any time of the year.

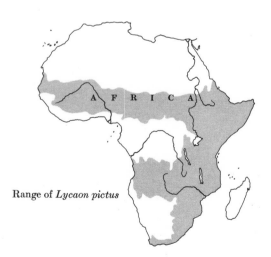

Range of *Lycaon pictus*

Range of *Ursus middendorffi*

Kodiak Bear

Ursus middendorffi

THE LARGEST LIVING FLESH EATER. The soft fur of this beautiful big animal which measures about 9 feet in length and may weigh up to 1,730 pounds is a magnificent trophy. But since the beast is shy and wary, it is not easy to hunt it; in spite of its bulk it is very agile, can run speedily over difficult terrain, catches wild, hoofed animals, swims well, and climbs trees but only when young. The range of the Kodiak or Alaskan brown bear is the Alaskan Peninsula, with the addition of several adjacent islands, notably Kodiak Island. It has a number of smaller relatives; the grizzly bear, for instance, and the Old World brown bear are only variations of the same species. The latter once inhabited most of Europe and Asia but is very rare now. The Kodiak bear hibernates during the winter and, like most other bears, feeds on laxative roots, mosses, and ants when it emerges from its shelter. Some of these bears are actually vegetarians while others enjoy a mixed diet of plant and animal material, and still others feed on meat only. Fish are also a desirable food; standing in an ice-cold glacial stream, the huge beast may remain in a completely motionless pose; then suddenly there is a lightning movement of the muzzle, and a big salmon is caught and carried ashore.

A LEGEND OF THE OLD WEST. Huge, vicious grizzly bears attacking hunters and lumberjacks were part of the Wild West story. More sober observations have shown that these big "silver-tipped" beasts avoid human contacts and run away unless provoked; yet they should be treated with great caution, for their strength is awe-inspiring. One 800-pound specimen, for instance, was once observed to attack, kill and drag to its den a 1000-pound buffalo. Up to a century ago grizzlies roamed the west of the continent from Alaska and Canada down to Mexico. Now they are rare in a wild state; some naturalists ascribe their decline, partly at least, to the disappearance of the bison herds which used to furnish much of their food. However, they have increased in numbers under protection in Yellowstone and Glacier National Parks. The grizzly, which does not represent a species by itself but a variation of the brown bear, has a head-and-body length of up to 8 feet, with a shoulder height of 5 feet and a weight of 800 pounds. It is omnivorous, with approximately the same diet as the Kodiak bear. During the fall it fattens up and with the advent of winter finds a cave or digs a cavity in a hillside for its hibernation; it will occupy this shelter during a heavy snowfall which obliterates all tracks leading to the den. Its winter sleep is not a true hibernation in the sense of that of some mammals whose body functions slow down and produce a lethargic state. All functions remain near normal and the bear is easily awakened. During that period the one to three cubs are born, weighing just a little over one pound each; they stay with their mother for at least a year.

Grizzly Bear

Ursus arctos

Range of *Ursus arctos*

THE GENUS BLACK BEAR MAY BE WHITE. It may also be dark brown, the color of chocolate; lighter brown, the color of cinnamon; or blue-black. White specimens are mostly encountered on the ranges of the Pacific coast, and blue-black ones in Alaska's St. Elias Mountains. Sometimes each of the two or three cubs which comprise a litter represent a different color phase. To heighten the confusion, the genus brown bear of the Old World may be black. The characteristic difference between the black bear (*Euarctos*) and the brown bear (*Ursus*) lies in their anatomy; the American black bear is smaller and its hind feet and its claws are shorter; its hair forms a more uniform blanket. When the first European settlers arrived in the New World, they encountered black bears in all the wooded areas of the continent, from northern Canada to central Mexico. Today the species is restricted to the more remote forest regions. Their numbers have greatly increased in the national parks of the United States and Canada where the animals have become accustomed to human handouts. Although park visitors are warned not to feed bears, many do so anyhow and every year accidents and injuries are reported. The bears are dangerous when cornered or when defending their cubs. The antics of the young are most amusing, and they learn various tricks quite easily. A few become circus performers riding bicycles and entertaining with similar acts. The head and body of an adult may measure up to 6 feet in length, with a shoulder height of three feet and a weight of up to 330 pounds. The diet includes meat, fish, carrion, and vegetable matter; if an opportunity presents itself they will kill a sheep or a hog. They fatten up during the fall and with the arrival of winter retire to a den where they hibernate; however, they break up their sleep with occasional wanderings during the periods of warmer weather which usually occur in winter. In January or February two or three small cubs are born to the female hibernating in a shelter.

Black Bear

Ursus americanus

Range of *Ursus americanus*

Polar Bear

Thalarctos maritimus

Range of *Thalarctos maritimus*

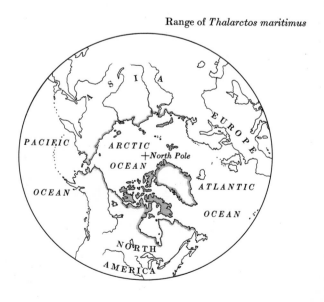

A GREAT ARCTIC NOMAD. The polar bear, which lives around the North Pole wherever there are seals in open water, is a long-distance traveler. Often it drifts on ice floes hundreds of miles away from land, catching seals, sea birds and fish. During the summer it may swim ashore at the southern rim of the Arctic Sea to eat the berries of tundra plants or to enjoy a meal of musk ox or reindeer. The Eskimos hunt it and use its fur and fat; the chase is dangerous and a vicious and hungry specimen may stalk, attack and kill a man. Its only other natural enemy seems to be the walrus. A big adult male may have a length of up to 8 feet with a shoulder height of 5 feet and a weight of 1600 pounds; females weigh only half of that. The white or yellowish fur covers also the soles of the bear's feet, offering protection against the cold and a more secure foothold on ice. Polar bears do not hibernate but the female digs a snow den for the birth of her one to four young in early spring; she takes care of them for one to two years.

Sloth Bear

Melursus ursinus

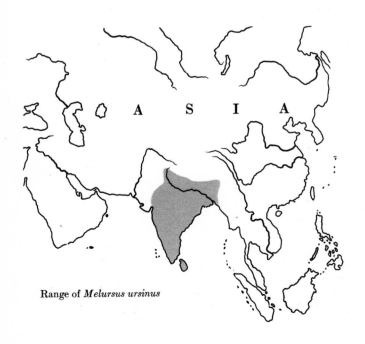

Range of *Melursus ursinus*

NOISY SLEEPER, NOISY EATER. When a sloth bear sleeps on the forest ground, he snores loudly. When he is at his favorite occupation of cleaning out a termite nest, his thunderous blowing, sucking, belching and puffing can be heard 600 feet away. He proceeds systematically: first, his powerful claws dig up the nest, then he cleans the place by blowing off the dust, and finally he sucks up the insects from the brood galleries. For this action he is well equipped; his naked and flexible lips protrude, his nostrils open and shut at will, and in place of the upper pair of incisors there is a gap in the front row of his teeth. These special anatomical features turn his snout into an effective vacuum cleaner. But termites are not his only food; like any bear he looks for honey, devours carrion, and feeds on eggs and vegetable matter. The range of the sloth bear, a single genus and species, covers the wooded parts of India but does not extend into the Himalaya; it is also fairly common in Ceylon. Its greatest head-and-body length is 6 feet, with a shoulder height of 3 feet and a weight of 300 pounds. The shaggy hair is black, sometimes mixed with gray, brown, or red. On its chest a white or yellowish mark has the shape of a V. Disliking roads and settlements, it keeps away from them; on the whole it is harmless, but the natives are afraid of it since some people have been mauled by sloth bears in a state of panic. The family life of this bear is close; couples seem to be monogamous, and both father and mother take care of the two or three cubs which stay with their parents for up to three years.

A "COON" AS NATIONAL EMBLEM? Some admirers of the raccoon advocate the dismissal of the bald eagle from the seal of the United States and the elevation of the little bear with the ring tail in its place. For the eagle, they say, is a parasite while the raccoon symbolizes the skillful, resourceful, tough but nimble, self-reliant American. It has a number of endearing traits. It washes its food in a running brook to clean it of dirt and grit, and it uses its little long-fingered hands as often as monkeys or human beings use them. Its footprint looks like the miniature of that of a man. The coon tail with its five to ten black rings adorned the cap of American frontiersmen, and in the South coon hounds had to be especially bred and trained to deal with this clever animal. The raccoon seems to be attracted by civilization, does not mind living near human settlements and is fond — it must be admitted — of raiding garbage cans. Its range extends from Canada to Central America; in the north it hibernates, but not in the south. The maximum head-and-body length is 2 feet, with a shoulder height of 1 foot and a weight of 5 pounds; its fur is gray to black, the eye patch and the rings on the furry tail are black. Hunting at night rather than by day, it thrives on an omnivorous diet of fish and frogs, small rodents, fruits and nuts. Its one to seven young will live to an age of approximately ten years.

Range of *Procyon lotor*

Raccoon

Procyon lotor

Giant Panda

Ailuropoda melanoleuca

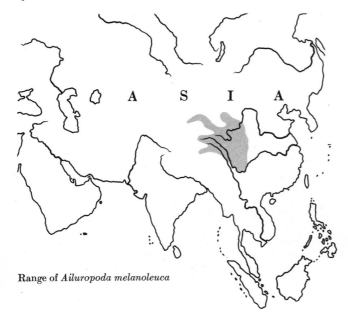

Range of *Ailuropoda melanoleuca*

A WORLD-FAMOUS RARITY. Although this is a very rare creature from a remote corner of the earth, it is widely known in the shape of a toy or as a picture-book animal. The few giant pandas living in zoological gardens are prime attractions and receive the publicity of celebrities. They look like bears in a clown's costume, and the entertaining antics of young pandas fit their grotesque appearance. The forested mountains of western China are their native range; during the summer they are also found in sections of the Tibetan plateau. To the Chinese the giant panda has been known since prehistoric times but the western world refused to accept such an absurd bear as anything but a myth. Not until the late 19th century was it scientifically described. Although it belongs to the order of meat eaters, it eats meat — small rodents, hares, fishes — only occasionally. The mainstay of its diet is bamboo shoots and roots, and

Range of *Mustela erminea*

Weasel

Mustela erminea

its forepaws are especially constructed for the grasping of the stems. Selected other plants and grasses are also acceptable. In captivity it is fed an entirely vegetarian diet. It attains a head-and-body length of 5 feet and a weight of 355 pounds; its thick coat is woolly, and the white parts become dirty in the course of years. It is a solitary animal which does not hibernate; it lives on the ground but will climb a tree to escape from hunting dogs. One or two cubs are born in caves, crevices or hollow tree shelters.

PEST OR BENEFACTOR? Fierce and lightning-quick, a tiny weasel will kill far beyond its food requirements, apparently just for the love of killing. A dozen chickens may be found dead in the coop, the weasel having entered through a knothole. On the other hand it is an excellent exterminator of vermin; it will rid a neighborhood of all destructive rodents for several hundred feet around, then start in a new territory elsewhere, hunting at night rather than by day. It is doubtful whether the world's rodent population could

be held to a tolerable level without the effective work of the weasels. They attack any animal up to the size of a rabbit and kill by a bite at the base of the skull. Their body is slender and wherever they can insert the head, the rest will slide through; in this way they can pursue rodents to the end of their burrows and trap them there. Some species will also climb trees, in the pursuit of squirrels. The range of the ten species is wide; in the New World it extends from Canada south to northern South America, and in the Old World throughout Europe and northern Africa, Asia and Indonesia. The natives of northern Burma are said to tame weasels and train them to kill geese and baby goats. Weasels will grow to a head-and-body length of 9¾ inches and to a weight of not quite three-quarters of a pound. Their summer coats are brown above and yellowish below; in the colder regions they change to white during the winter and furnish the fur for the ermine coats of royal coronations. They have one litter per year, with not less than three and sometimes as many as 13 young.

Eastern Mink

Mustela vison

Range of *Mustela vison*

MARK OF ELEGANCE. Mink garments, once a luxury for the very rich, are coming into more general use; a flourishing breeding industry has been developed which has caused a lowering of the price of the pelts. On the North American mink ranches the breeding stock is usually a cross between the Alaskan variety, because of its large body, and the Labrador type, because of its dark color. These ranches which also have created, through the use of mutations, strains in platinum and other rare shades, provide almost one-half of the pelts that reach the market. Of the two species of this valuable furbearer the New World mink is a native of Alaska, Canada, and the United States while the Old World mink lives in eastern Europe and Asia. Both species are dark brown. They attain a head-and-body length of up to 21 inches and a weight of up to 3½ pounds. Quick and fierce, these mainly nocturnal hunters catch small animals on land or in streams or lakes; frogs and fish are included in their menu. They are the only members of the genus *Mustela* which are as much land-bound as water-bound. Four to ten young are born in a nest in an abandoned muskrat house, or a small cave in a riverbank, or under a shelter of rocks.

WILD AND TAME. In the American countryside the term "polecat" is sometimes applied to the skunk. This however, is a misnomer; the true bearer of that name is the European polecat, with related forms in northern Africa and Asia. Its fur is dark brown or black, with yellowish spots on each side of the face between the eye and the ear; the pelt used to be a popular fur known as "fitch." Its head-and-body length may reach 20 inches, and it weighs up to 3 pounds. Five to eight young are bred twice a year; they are reared only by the mother. The polecat makes a pleasant pet; in fact, a domesticated strain has been derived from it, the so-called ferret, whose fur is usually white. Ferrets are kept to kill rats and flush rabbits out of their holes, for the benefit of the hunter. In former centuries ferrets were sometimes trained together with falcons to aid in the rabbit chase. The polecat has an American relative which belongs to the same sub-genus, the black-footed ferret, a native of western North America. Its fur color is yellowish but its eye patch, tail tip and feet are black. It is the arch enemy of the prairie dog; not only does it "ferret" these rodents from their burrows and eat them but it also uses their holes as shelter. Both the ferret and the prairie dog have the same range.

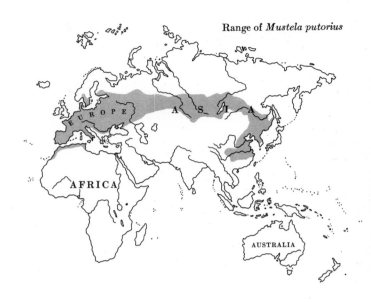

Range of *Mustela putorius*

European Polecat

Mustela putorius

A FUR FOR KINGS. For centuries, unsurpassed beauty and softness made sable the favorite fur of royalty. It still is a high-priced luxury article, and attempts to breed martens (the genus which produces "sable") have largely failed. For these high-strung, restless animals so far have refused to mate in captivity, and research will have to determine the right environmental conditions which may induce a few couples to breed; from such beginnings breeding colonies could be established. True sable is the fur of the Siberian marten which is trapped on the mountain ranges between the Urals and Kamchatka; altogether about six species are found in Europe and Asia. The pelts of the two American species, the fisher and the American marten, are sold as "American sable," but only those furs which are almost black; the golden-brown ones are just "marten," and come from Alaska, Canada, and the northern United States. All the members of the genus *Martes* are largely arboreal, solitary, shy, wary, and hunt and travel day or night, summer and winter. They eat small rodents, especially squirrels, carrion, insects and fruits. The fisher seems to have a predilection for porcupines which he turns over with a sudden blow; then he tears open the belly; even young deer, immobilized in deep snow, have been attacked by martens. Head-and-body length varies between just over 1 foot and 2 feet, and weight between 1½ and 4½ pounds. One to five young are born in a hollow tree den, preferably in a coniferous forest.

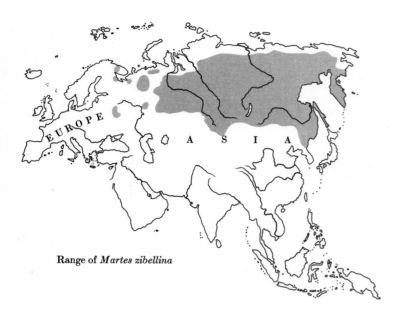

Range of *Martes zibellina*

Eurasian Sable

Martes zibellina

Tayra

Tayra barbara

"CABEZA DE VIEJO" - *"HEAD OF AN OLD MAN."* That's what the Mexicans call the tayra. The Central Americans rather see a resemblance with a dog; their name for the tayra is *perrito ligero* - "fast small dog." Another Latin American localism is *comadreja grande* - "big godmother," referring to a folklorical town character who is vivacious, active and gossipy. These round-eared, long-legged relatives of the martens form a single species of the genus and are natives of the Latin American countries from Mexico south to Argentina and Paraguay. They are agile runners, swimmers and climbers and have a special method of eluding pursuing dogs. At first they run on the ground for a stretch; suddenly they climb up a tree and for several hundred feet jump from branch to branch; then they are back on earth again and repeat the sequence, utterly confusing the dogs. The tayra's shorthaired body fur is brown or black, the head brown, gray, or black; a white or yellowish patch decorates the chest. Their feet have naked soles and strong claws. The odor they emit is described as pleasant by some and obnoxious by others. Their head and body is up to 2 feet 3 inches long, and they may weigh up to 10 pounds. Small mammals—rabbits, squirrels, even young deer—are their principal food, as well as birds. They also like fruit and sometimes raid banana plantations. Two to four young are born in a hollow tree.

Range of *Tayra barbara*

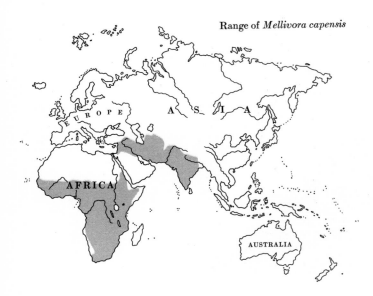

Range of *Mellivora capensis*

A USEFUL PARTNERSHIP. This badger, also called "ratel," loves honey; so does a little African bird named the "honey guide." The latter knows where the wild beehives are but cannot get at them; so it utters a special call and guides the honey badger to the hives. The nests are ripped open and bird and badger feast on honey. This small but strong animal whose range includes Africa south of the Sahara and Asia from Arabia and Turkestan to Nepal and India is a remarkable species in other respects also. Its skin is so tough that dog-bites, porcupine-quills, bee-stings and snake-bites cannot pierce it; it is so incredibly loose that it just hangs on the body. When a dog seizes a honey badger by its neck, the latter is by no means incapacitated; it twists around inside the skin and bites the dog. Its eating habits are unusual; its omnivorous diet includes insects and small mammals, amphibians and carrion; it also thrives on poisonous cobras. When it kills a sheep, it shows a selective taste; first it will eat tongue and eyes, windpipe and brain, then it will rip open the body and devour the intestines. Although not large — it has a head-and-body length of up to 2½ feet, with a shoulder height of not quite one foot — it attacks an intruder and badly wounds even horses and buffaloes. Its front claws are excellent digging tools, and it secretes a stinking fluid as a deterrent. Its coarse coat is unique. The dark brown or black underparts are covered with what seems to be a white or yellow blanket. Two honey badger young are born in hollow trees, burrows, or crevices.

Honey Badger

Mellivora capensis

American Badger

Taxidea taxus

A MASTER DIGGER. On the dry, open plains of southwestern Canada and the western and central United States, way down into Mexico, the American badger lives a largely nocturnal life digging its livelihood from the earth. It digs pocket gophers, prairie dogs and other rodents out of their burrows, and in case of danger it quickly digs itself into the ground, working frantically with its four claws. To fashion a nest for its one to five, usually two young, it may burrow a hole thirty feet deep, and if it catches a prey too big to be eaten at one meal, for instance a rabbit, it may drag the carcass into its dugout and stay with it for several days, as long as the food lasts. The large badger holes are often appropriated as shelters and nesting sites by other animals but are not appreciated by the ranchers whose cattle and horses are sometimes hurt in the hazardous excavations. The badger is therefore hunted and destroyed although it is a valuable killer of rodents. A solitary plains-dweller, it may attain a head-and-body length of 2½ feet and a weight of 22 pounds. Its coat grows especially long hair of grayish-reddish color on both sides, and a white stripe runs from the nose to the shoulders; the underparts are yellowish, the feet black or dark brown. The skin is extremely tough and hangs loosely around its body, which enables the badger to wriggle out of tight spots. While it does not exactly hibernate, it has spells of long sleep in the north, as long as the soil is frozen. Badger pelts have a limited acceptance in the fur industry, and for decades badger hair was used in shaving brushes but it is now replaced by plastic materials.

Range of *Taxidea taxus*

Striped Skunk

Mephitis mephitis

Range of *Mephitis mephitis*

THE CHEMICAL WEAPON. The skunk is peace-loving, self-confident and indifferent to human beings and other animals. But when it is too badly annoyed it takes a stand. It stamps its forefeet, raises the tail, and finally lifts its posterior and swings it to the front so that head and rear form a U. From two glands under the tail it squirts a yellowish, strongly scented, oily fluid which as a mist hits the target, usually the eyes of the adversary. The attack can be repeated six times before the chemical ammunition is temporarily exhausted. The liquid contains a skin-burning sulfide which causes temporary blindness and nausea. The common or striped skunk has a wide range which stretches from southern Canada to northern Mexico; its relative, the hooded skunk, occurs from the southwestern United States through Central America. The striped skunk derives its name from a white stripe which runs over the top of the head and then separates into two stripes on the back but there is considerable variation in the black and white color pattern. Head-and-body length may reach 15 inches, with a weight of 5½ pounds. The four to ten, usually four or five young are born in a den, in a burrow or under a building. In the north, skunks sleep through the winter, with a few outdoor excursions. They are omnivorous and valuable destroyers of Japanese beetles, potato bugs, and other harmful insects, and of vermin.

PLAYFUL ACROBAT. These handsome little skunks are among the sprightliest forest dwellers. Playing among themselves, they run upside down on their forefeet, keeping their raised bodies in a well-balanced vertical position — a hilarious sight. They can also climb trees with ease. The range of the eastern species shown here extends through the southeastern and central parts of the United States. The spotted skunk's head and body may be a foot long, with a weight of up to 2¼ pounds. Its fur — the finest of the various genera of skunks — has a highly variable color pattern of white stripes and spots on a black background. The beautiful white-plumed tail serves as a warning signal to a potential attacker. When it is suddenly erected, the anal glands are about to spray the strongly smelling misty secretion at the enemy and will temporarily blind and incapacitate him. The spotted skunk's diet includes plant material and insects during the summer and small mammals, especially rodents, during the winter. The annual litters — two in the south, one in the north, consists of two to six, usually four or five young; their plant-lined dens are normally underground but sometimes high up in trees. Being nocturnal, the animals sleep during the day, and outside of the mating season seven or eight skunks will sometimes share the same shelter.

Range of *Spilogale putorius*

Spotted Skunk

Spilogale putorius

Canadian Otter

Lutra canadensis

Range of *Lutra canadensis*

THE DELIGHTS OF RIVER LIFE. River otters are expert swimmers; their feet are webbed, and since they can close their ears and nostrils, they are able to stay under water for long periods, hunting for fish and frogs, crayfish and turtles. Ashore they catch small animals. Truly playful, they slide down mud banks and snow chutes, and when the slides are tunneled through deep snow, the fun is doubled. Their range is worldwide. River otters occur in the lakes, streams, and estuaries of every continent except Australia; twelve species are distinguished but they resemble each other closely. Their greatest head-and-body length is 2 feet 7 inches, with a weight of up to 31 pounds. Their upper parts are brownish, their lower parts lighter; their dense and durable fur is used for coat trimmings.

THE COMFORTS OF LIFE AT SEA. Normally this fascinating animal spends its days floating on its back, using its chest as a tray or table on which it piles its food — crabs, sea urchins, and mollusks. Exceptionally intelligent, it employs a tool to prepare its meals. It keeps a stone on its chest on which it breaks the shells of clams, mussels and snails. Sometimes it plays a ball game, tossing a shell back and forth between its hands. A female keeps her single young on her chest where it is fed and groomed. At night the sea otter sleeps under strands of kelp so it will not drift away; sometimes it holds its forepaws over its eyes. Up to the 18th century its range extended from Lower California to Alaska and the Aleutians in American waters and along the Kamchatka Peninsula in Asian waters. But because of its dense and beautiful fur it was hunted almost to extinction; since the early 20th century it is protected and has increased in numbers but today's colonies in California and Alaska, the Kurils and the Commander Islands represent only 20 percent of the original range. The coastal waters with a depth of 10 to 65 feet are its habitat; it rarely ventures farther out to sea than two-thirds of a mile, and only a few yards on land. The sea otter grows to a head-and-body length of up to 4 feet, and males attain a weight of up to 82 pounds. The coat is dark brown or black, and lighter below.

Range of *Enhydra lutris*

Sea Otter

Enhydra lutris

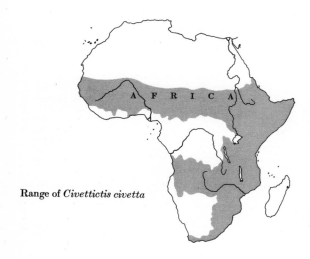

Range of *Civettictis civetta*

African Civet

Civettictis civetta

THE SCENTS OF AFRICA. King Solomon procured the perfume for his wives from Ethiopia; the aromatic substance had been extracted from the African civet, an animal that lived and still lives south of a line from Senegal in West Africa to Somaliland in East Africa. Interestingly, the method of preparing the civet's valuable cosmetic product is still the same as it was in King Solomon's day, three thousand years ago. African natives, particularly in Ethiopia, catch a number of specimens and keep them in sturdy stockades; several times a week they extract the musk from the civet's anal glands, obtaining an average weekly yield of three to five grams. The animals are not domesticated — seemingly they are untamable — or raised in captivity; whenever the need arises, new wild civets are trapped. The musk with the strong and pleasant smell is packed in cow horns which find their way to the world's perfume industry; the substance is an excellent fixative and base for other essences. The civet, a single species, attains a head-and-body length of up to 2 feet. Its long-haired, coarse coat is black with a pattern of white or yellow stripes and patches. All four feet are equipped with claws and hairy soles. A nocturnal mammal, it likes to travel through dense brushlands where it hunts for its mixed animal-vegetable food; occasionally it invades corn fields and raids chicken coops. Although a typical land animal, it swims well and in an emergency climbs trees. A coughing sound is said to be its call; when confronted with danger, it is reported to utter a deep growl while the hair on its body stands on end. Two annual litters are the rule, each consisting of two to three young.

African Mongoose

Herpestes ichneumon

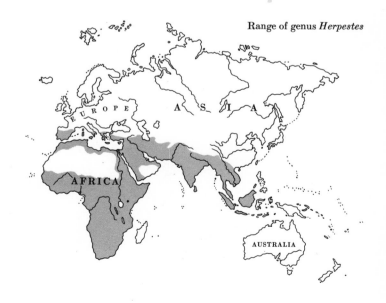

Range of genus *Herpestes*

A LIGHTNING-SPEED KILLER. Some forms of the genus *Herpestes*, the true mongooses, have become known as the arch-foes of cobras and other venomous snakes. They are not immune to serpentine poison but are so quick and have such an innate knowledge of snake behavior that they practically always win the fight. They induce the cobra to strike, turn aside, seize it by the head, crack the skull and eat the snake. They also feed on small mammals, amphibians, birds and insects. The approximately eight species of the genus inhabit a belt from southern Europe eastward to India and Malaysia, and throughout Africa. Introduced to the West Indies and the Hawaiian Islands in order to end local rat plagues, they have become pests there. They have exterminated not only the rats but also all other small mammals and have seriously reduced the bird population. Consequently there is an embargo on importing mongooses to the United States. The largest members of the genus grow to a length of 2 feet 1 inch, with a weight of 7 pounds.

Spotted Hyena

Crocuta crocuta

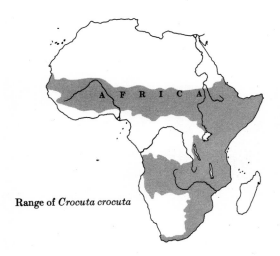

Range of *Crocuta crocuta*

BONE CRUSHER. Of all living animals the spotted hyena probably possesses the most powerful jaws, for its size. It crushes the leg bones of a buffalo, a hippo or elephant as if they were matches. Running in packs at a speed of up to 40 mph it roams the countryside in search of carrion, and for centuries it cleaned up the tribal battlefields by eating the dead warriors. It also attacks goats, sheep, or any animal it can overpower but has a reputation of being a coward; it runs away in case of a counterattack. Occasionally it has carried off sleeping children. Its blood-curdling howls, increasing in volume and rising in pitch, and its insane-sounding "laughter" — a sign of excitement — are among the voices of the African night in the hyena's range, south of the Sahara. The spotted hyena attains a head-and-body length of about 5 feet, with a shoulder height of 2½ feet and a weight of up to 182 pounds; the coarse fur is yellowish-gray with dark round spots. Externally the reproductive organs of males and females look so much alike that the ancient world thought of these animals as hermaphrodites.

SCAVENGER AND GRAVE DIGGER. All hyenas — the spotted, the striped and the rare brown species — are scavengers and in certain sections of their ranges act as a sanitation corps. In the evening, villagers place their domestic garbage on the street, and the next morning the refuse is cleaned up; the hyenas have been there during the night. The striped hyena is smaller than its spotted relative and has a different range which extends from Asia Minor eastward to Russian Central Asia, Afghanistan, West Pakistan, and India. Its head-and-body length is about 4 feet, with a maximum weight of 120 pounds. Its coarse coat is grayish-yellowish-brownish with dark brown or black markings. The tracks of its forefeet are considerably larger than those of its hind feet, and a hyena trail can be readily recognized. It prefers carrion, and even if the vultures have cleaned all meat from a carcass, the hyena still feeds on the bones which it crushes with ease. It also attacks small animals, is known to have carried off little children, and occasionally digs up human burials. Normally it avoids a fight; when in danger it growls and erects its mane. Its litter consists of four to six, usually two to four young which are born in a cave or a den among rocks; their life span is approximately 24 years.

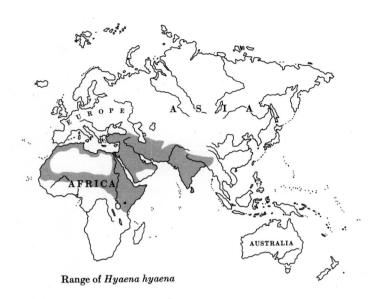

Range of *Hyaena hyaena*

Striped Hyena

Hyaena hyaena

Canada Lynx

Lynx canadensis

Range of *Lynx canadensis*

HUNTER OF THE WINTRY FOREST. Because of its range which includes Alaska, Canada and the northern United States, this native cat is well-equipped for life in a cold climate. Its long, strong legs and big furred feet are designed for travel over snowy ground. A speedy swimmer, a skillful climber of trees, and a savage fighter attacking with both claws and teeth, the Canada lynx devours any animal or bird it can overpower; on its nightly travels which may cover a route of 25 miles, it can pull down even a young deer. Sometimes it may kill a sheep or raid a chicken coop but on the whole it is beneficial to farming because it destroys rodents. In its northern range the snow hare is its principal food, to such an extent that the lynx population rises and falls with the cycle of the snow hare population. In times of scarcity of hares, the lynxes will travel far beyond their regular range. Head and body may reach a length of 3 feet, with a weight of 25 pounds; the coloration of its fur is grayish mottled with brown. Characteristic features are the long-haired ruff around the neck and the ear tufts. The one to four young are born in a cave or in a den prepared in a thicket or on a rocky ledge. Close relatives which belong to the same genus are the European lynx, the bobcat of North America, and the caracal of Africa and southern Asia.

WHICH ARE THE ANCESTORS OF THE HOUSE CAT? Wild cats resembling our domestic breeds are found in many parts of the world. Exactly how this wild stock developed into the tame house cat is not known but it is assumed that early man tamed the native species of his region, that the cats followed him as pets on his travels, and mated with other species in other areas. Today the resulting mixture can no longer be traced to its origins. Interest in domesticating cats probably arose when man turned from hunting to farming, began to grow and store grain and appreciated the cat's skill in catching mice and other destructive vermin. In ancient Egypt cats were not only tamed, some 3,300 years ago, but also worshiped as god-like creatures. The cat goddess, Bast, protected hunters, lovers, and pleasure seekers, and in the city of Bubastis the veneration of cats had become the accepted religion. One of the wild species that looks like a domestic breed is the sand cat whose range encompasses northern Africa including the Sahara, Arabia, and the south of Russian Central Asia. Its soft fur is sandy-colored with dark markings on legs and tail; ears, paws, and chin are white. It is a desert animal, and its sand color seems to represent a protective mimicry; however, since it sleeps in holes or crevices during the day and ventures out only in the dark of night, the purpose of the color adaptation is not known.

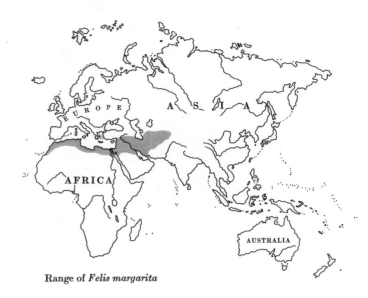

Range of *Felis margarita*

Sand Cat

Felis margarita

LEAPS AND BOUNDS. The serval is the fastest-leaping cat, incredibly speedy at short distances. It is able to perform a unique hunting feat. It flushes a bird on the ground and a second later catches it in the air, by leaping more quickly than the bird can fly away. On a different occasion an African starling or any other bird may feel perfectly safe when perched on a branch ten feet above the ground; but with a sudden leap the serval will catch it. Small mammals which seek refuge in a tree are regularly captured; for the serval is a sure and rapid climber. If a dog starts a fight, the serval usually kills it. No wonder, then, that robes made of serval pelts are worn by tribal chiefs and leaders, in the primitive belief that the animal's courage and skill will be magically transferred to the wearer of the fur. The serval's range is Africa, particularly equatorial Africa; forests and especially natural meadows of tall grass are its habitat. This long-legged, short-tailed cat with the slender, sloping form attains a head-and-body length of 3 feet; its fur is yellowish-brown on its back and sides, and much lighter beneath; the rather sparse and diffuse spots are dark brown or black. Since its ears are large and its eyes bright, it is able to hunt either by day or night; its diet consists of birds, small mammals, lizards and insects. For its young it builds a den or form in the thick, tall grass.

Range of *Felis serval*

Serval

Felis serval

Fishing Cat

Felis viverrina

ASIATIC FISHERMAN. All cats like fish but this species of southern and southeastern Asia makes a specialty of fishing. Living in forests, grasslands and marshlands it visits the shores of streams and lakes, skillfully catches fish and eats them. However, fish is not its only food; it also hunts for birds and small mammals. It has a head-and-body length of up to 2½ feet; dull gray is the ground color of its fur, the spots are dark. The fishing cat and the other small species of wild cats of the genus *Felis* have a number of traits in common with our domestic cats. They are only a little larger and like the same kind of food; the females have one or more litters per year, each consisting of one to six, normally two to four young (the domestic breeds may have more); the mothers bring food to their kittens and teach them to hunt. One odor which stirs and excites all these cats, both the wild and the domestic ones, is that of catnip; they try to catch the source of the smell, i.e., the plant itself, roll on it, rub it on their fur and purr happily. One interesting relative of the fishing cat is the steppe or Pallas' cat (*Felis manul*) which according to some experts may be the ancestor of our beautiful long-haired Persian cat. It occurs in rocky areas of Central Asia, and its thick fur, doubly long on the underparts, protects it against the snowy and frozen ground. The coloration is almost white, with a few black markings.

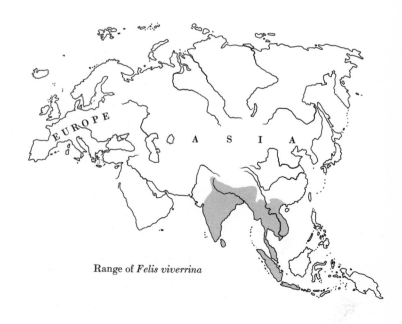

Range of *Felis viverrina*

Ocelot

Felis pardalis

Range of *Felis pardalis*

NIGHT HUNT IN THE TREETOPS. This handsome cat is an excellent climber and at night roams through the branches of trees catching and killing monkeys and tree rats, porcupines and lizards; it also hunts on the ground, dashing through the tall grass after birds and small animals, including poultry and livestock. A New World cat, at one time abundant in our Southwest, it is still found there, but only rarely. It is more common in South America, as far south as northern Argentina and Paraguay. Its habitat are the forest and scrublands of the warmer regions of the continent. Head-and-body length of a male adult is 2½ to 3 feet with a tail half that long. Its fur is quite valuable, for its color pattern is spectacular; the head and neck are adorned with dark bars on a tawny background, the back and the flanks with dark rings. All these markings are arranged in chain-like bands. The limbs show blotches, and the underparts are whitish. Bands circle the tail. This cat has the habit of leaving its droppings at certain spots where heaps accumulate, apparently to mark its own territory. South American natives sometimes keep young ocelots as pets; but the animals become unruly and dangerous when they reach adulthood.

AN AMERICAN WILDCAT. This native of the New World, with a name from the Guaraní language, is not much larger than a domestic cat. Its main characteristic, besides its narrow face, is its plain coat which lacks rings, spots or bars. One color phase of the species is dark gray, occasionally almost black, while the other is reddish. It inhabits the forest, particularly its edges, and the so-called chaparral from the Mexican border of the United States south to northern Argentina. This short-legged cat has a head-and-body length of approximately 26 inches, with a long tail measuring about 23 inches. Solitary by nature, the males and females hardly ever see each other except in the mating season, and the males show no interest in their offspring. They hunt on the ground rather than in the trees, birds being their favorite food. Latin American folklore endows them with an almost supernatural skill in raiding chicken coops; they are said to sense the right time and occasion so that they are never caught.

Range of *Felis yagouaroundi*

Jaguarundi
Felis yagouaroundi

Puma

Felis concolor

Range of
Felis concolor

MOUNTAIN LION, PUMA, COUGAR, CATA-MOUNT. This multiplicity of names for a single species indicates the important role it plays in American lore — usually a dangerous and sinister role. In fact, however, the puma is a shy and retiring beast, does not stage unprovoked attacks on man and lives largely on birds and small mammals although deer and other game are also pulled down. Some marauders develop a taste for livestock — sheep, goats, and calves — and break into pastures; they should be shot, but no general campaign against the mountain lion would be justified; as it is, its numbers have been greatly reduced by hunters. Up to a century ago the puma's range encompassed all of North and South America. Today it is restricted to the western part of the double continent and extends from British Columbia to Patagonia. This is still the widest range of any native American mammal. The puma is a large animal, attaining a head-and-body length of a little over 6 feet with a weight of up to 233 pounds. Its fur is yellowish-brownish above and pale below. The young are spotted and have a ringed tail but gradually lose their markings.

THE KILLER WHICH OVERCOMES ITS PREY IN A SINGLE BOUND. That is said to be the meaning of the word *jaguar* in the Indian languages of South America. Most Latin Americans call the animal *el tigre* which, of course, is incorrect. The jaguar's range extends from the southwestern regions of the United States southward through Central and South America to central Chile and Argentina. It is encountered in various habitats, in arid shrub country, in thick woods, on dry mountain terrain and in the wet jungles of the Amazon Basin. It is a good swimmer and also a skillful climber of trees, especially in the Amazon river system where the forest floor is frequently flooded. The head-and-body length of the jaguar is approximately 6 feet, with a weight of up to 300 pounds. The fur is buff with black rings or rosettes which show a black spot in the center. Its diet consists mostly of smaller mammals like peccaries and capybaras but also of fish, turtles, and even alligators. Occasionally ranches are raided and domestic livestock is killed. But while among the other large cats of the genus *Panthera* dangerous man-eaters develop now and then, no similar cases are known for the jaguar. Its litters consist of one to three young which have a life expectancy of 15 to 30 years.

Range of
Panthera onca

Jaguar
Panthera onca

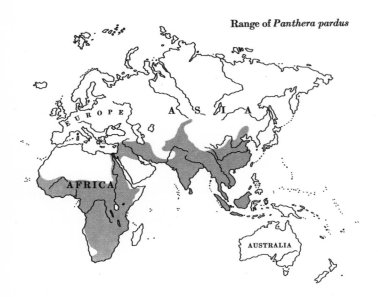

Range of *Panthera pardus*

DEATH FROM ABOVE. Leopards, the most cunning and silent of the big cats, like to live, sleep and mate in trees; from an overhanging branch they may suddenly drop on a passing prey and kill it instantly. The meat they cannot devour on the spot is dragged up a tree and stored in a "pantry" of forked branches; it will provide a meal on the following day. Any animal the leopard can overpower will be eaten, especially birds and monkeys. The leopard's range is larger than that of any other cat, comprising most of Africa (excepting the deserts) and most of Asia. At one time it occurred also in Europe but now it is extinct there. It is adaptable to climate and environment and lives in equatorial jungles, dry grasslands, rocky areas and on the cold plateaus of the Himalaya. Its head-and-body length may reach 5 feet, with a weight of 200 pounds. Its handsome buff coat with black rosettes is, unfortunately, a desirable pelt for the fur industry, and overhunting has severely reduced the leopard population. The "black panther" is not a separate species but merely a color phase of the leopard; in any single litter one young may be black.

Leopard

Panthera pardus

Siberian Tiger

Panthera tigris longipilis

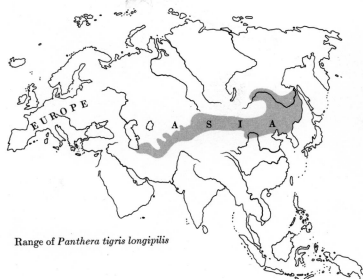

Range of *Panthera tigris longipilis*

THE MOST MAGNIFICENT CAT. The range of the tiger is enormous, reaching from the Arctic circle to the Equator. The species had to adapt itself to extreme differences in climate and environment, and the variety living in the far north turned out to be its most handsome and largest representative, measuring up to 10 feet in length. In accordance with the harsh surroundings of northern Asia, the Siberian tiger wears a coat of very long, pale outside fur over a thick undercoat, a warm protection against the icy winds of the Altay Mountains and the two thousand miles of inhospitable forest lands that reach across the northern waste. It keeps out of man's sight; a great traveler, it eats anything it can kill, including the numerous small rodents of the region.

A SHY, RESPLENDENT KILLER. At the circus spectacles of ancient Rome the lions were the leading performers, not the tigers; tigers were tried but declined to fight before a crowd. Indian maharajas who pitted tigers against wild water buffaloes had the same experience. In their regular habitat, as well, tigers usually avoid potential adversaries including man. At the same time they are skillful providers of food for themselves; stealthily they crawl through the jungle and, when in striking distance, kill their victim with a leap, a hug, and a bite. They devour almost any kind of animal including leopards; some individuals have cannibalistic instincts and eat other tigers, including their own young. On occasion they are reported to consume fish, turtles and crocodiles in addition. All of them like to bathe frequently; they are also able to climb trees. Of the various races the so-called royal Bengal tiger is the most common and best-known; it lives in the forests and marshy jungles of India, the Malay Peninsula, Sumatra, Java and Bali. An adult male may reach a head-and-body length of 9 feet, with a weight of 600 pounds. On the fur's ground color which varies from reddish-orange to white, the design of black stripes shows a different pattern on each side. The total impression is one of superb animalistic beauty which makes the tiger a star attraction in zoological gardens and circus acts. Of the litters of several cubs usually two survive; they stay with their mother for a year.

Tiger

Panthera tigris tigris

Range of
Panthera tigris tigris

KING OF BEASTS? His appearance is indeed awe-inspiring, his roar is disturbing, and his demeanor royal. In the great African preserves he seems to eye with tolerant contempt the tourists who pass by in landrovers. He may make a kill twice a week, but immediately afterwards the zebras and antelopes peacefully graze around his resting place. Family scenes are often charming: a lioness and her cubs fondle and hug each other most affectionately when she returns from the chase. Lions hunt singly, in pairs, or in "prides," with males and females, young and old taking part. Their strength lies in the initial spurt; with a few crushing leaps they descend on their prey, usually a hoofed animal. They are not very persevering runners and rest and sleep for long periods every day. Some become marauders and kill domestic livestock, and a few turn into dangerous man-eaters. A male lion may attain a head-and-body length of up to 8 feet and a weight of 500 pounds.

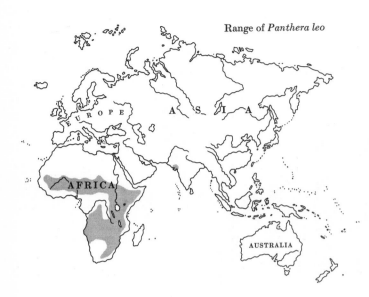

Range of *Panthera leo*

Lion

Panthera leo

His fur is dusty-yellow, with a dark-colored mane around his neck and shoulders. The species is polygamous and litters of one to six, usually two or three, are born at any time of the year. The range originally extended from Africa eastward to and including India; it is now restricted to the more protected grasslands and savannas of the African continent and the Gir forest in western India. Lions are not in danger of extinction; during World War II when sporting activities ceased and the male population went on war duty, they multiplied rapidly and became a pest; lions even strayed into the streets of Nairobi. In captivity they breed readily and are relatively inexpensive on the animal market.

A BEAUTIFUL JUNGLE CAT. The design of its fur is striking. On a grayish-yellowish background it wears unusual black markings in the form of boxes, spots, circles, rosettes, squares, ovals and other shapes; its long, luxurious tail is irregularly ringed. These markings are not present at birth but gradually appear as the animal grows up. Its range extends from Nepal south to Malaysia, Sumatra and Borneo, and east to southern China and Formosa. The clouded leopard has a head-and-body length of up to 3½ feet, with a weight of up to 51 pounds. It lives largely in trees, catches its prey by jumping from overhanging branches or hunts on the ground; its diet includes a great many animals from birds and monkeys to deer and cattle. It does not attack human beings. Not much is known about its habits in the wild but in captivity it is both affectionate and playful; it is fond of being petted and likes to toss some small object back and forth.

Clouded Leopard

Neofelis nebulosa

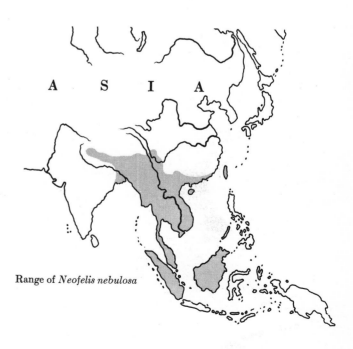

Range of *Neofelis nebulosa*

Snow Leopard

Uncia uncia

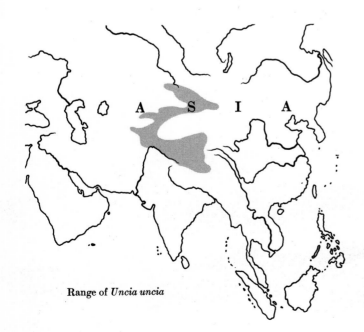

Range of *Uncia uncia*

A SPLENDID MOUNTAIN CAT. This leopard is seldom seen by human eyes, for it lives in the inaccessible mountain wilderness of central Asia, above the treeline at heights of between 11,000 and 12,500 feet; during the winter it descends to a level of approximately 6,000 feet. In Kashmir, Tibet, Russia and China it is encountered at such mountain massifs as the Himalaya, the Pamir, the Tien Shan and the Altay Mountains. It has a head-and-body length of up to 5 feet, a thickly furred tail of 3 feet, and a weight of up to 90 pounds. Over a dense undercoat it wears a rich, long-haired fur coat which is white with grayish or creamy shades on the upper parts and has a design of black rosettes of diffuse shapes; it is highly prized by the fur industry. The snow leopard sleeps during the day and hunts at night; the animals of the high-mountain fauna are its prey, especially hares and rodents, wild mountain sheep and musk deer, yaks and goats. Its litters consist of two to four young. The natives trap them, and the specimens delivered to our zoological gardens often have a toe or a foot missing, the result of traps. A more humane method is the digging of a pit with a narrow opening on top and a wide bottom.

THE SWIFTEST RUNNER ON EARTH. The cheetah is the speed champion of all mammals; for short distances it is able to run at the rate of 68 miles per hour. Hunters in India have made use of the cheetah's swiftness for centuries; they employ the animal in big game chases. A hood is placed over the cheetah's head and removed when the prey is in sight, the method used in falconry. The cheetah runs down the game, pulls it to the ground and waits for the master to kill it; it is rewarded with the victim's blood. From India the range extends westward to Egypt and north Africa; in tropical Africa the cheetah occurs south of a line from Nigeria in the west to Somaliland in the east; its habitat is the open country. It is superbly equipped for speed; because of its long legs it has a shoulder height of 3¼ feet with a head-and-body length of 5 feet, and may weigh up to 144 pounds. Its fur is white below and buff or grayish above, with a pattern of solid black spots. Its feet are rather dog-like than cat-like, with blunt claws which can be retracted only in part. Its diet consists of smaller gazelles, antelopes and similar prey. Depending upon the occasion, the cheetah produces a bird-like chirp, a barking sound, or, when pleased, a low purr.

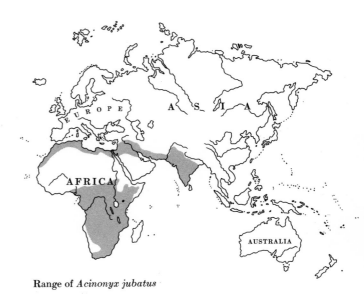

Range of *Acinonyx jubatus*

Cheetah

Acinonyx jubatus

Range of *Zalophus californianus*

THE MOST INTELLIGENT PINNIPED. Since this aquatic hunter is inquisitive, gregarious and playful by nature, it has been possible to train it for circus and vaudeville acts; it enjoys greatly showing off its ability to balance any object on its nose and to perform other tricks. It is a dweller of the Pacific, inhabiting the west coast of North America, the Galápagos Islands, and the southern part of the Sea of Japan. A male will grow to a length of 7¾ feet, with a weight of up to 620 pounds while the females are considerably smaller. Its fur is brown but appears black when it is wet. With great agility the animal hunts for squid, shellfish, octopus, herring and similar fish. Each June the bulls go ashore on a sandy or rocky beach or on the reef of an island, proceeding on their flippers, and wait for the cows to arrive; each bull keeps a harem of five to 20 mates whom he breeds after the pups have been born. They get acquainted with aquatic life in tidal pools, then accompany their mothers out to sea. The sea lions' barking can be heard on numerous points of the California coast.

California Sea Lion

Zalophus californianus

Northern Fur Seal

Callorhinus ursinus

A GREAT TRAVELER. During their wanderings these seals may cover as many as 5,800 miles a year. In winter and spring they are encountered from the southern Bering Sea to the southern California coast, in Siberia's Sea of Okhotsk and the southern part of the Sea of Japan. But for the summer and fall they all congregate on the Pribilofs and a few other islands of the far north for the mating season. There the huge bulls, up to 7 feet long and weighing perhaps 660 pounds, lord it over the females which are much smaller. The strongest and most savage males gather harems of up to 40 cows, and the business of delivering the pups and of breeding, a few days later, goes on in a bedlam of barking and coughing, roaring and bawling. Every few days the cows swim out to sea, sometimes for over a hundred miles, to feed on squid and fish; when they return they find without fail their own single young among thousands of pups. The bulls don't eat during this period. Their coloration is gray or brown above and reddish-brown below. Because their pelts are highly prized, they were overhunted to the point of extinction. Today an international treaty regulates the annual kill.

Range of *Callorhinus ursinus*

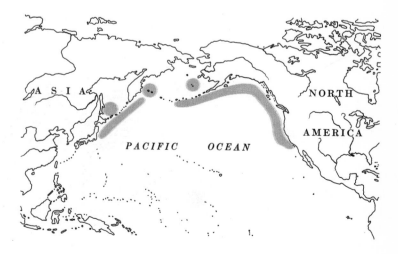

Range of *Odobenus rosmarus*

Walrus

Odobenus rosmarus

THE WHALE HORSE OF THE VIKINGS. The word *walrus* means "whale horse" in the Scandinavian languages, and the scientific name of the family, *Odobenidae,* may be translated as "creatures that walk with their teeth." This description refers to a peculiarity of the walrus: it uses its tusks for pulling its body onto an ice floe and off again on the opposite side, or for dragging itself over land. This is quite a chore for a 12-foot male who may weigh 1.2 metric tons. The tusks, about three feet long, may also serve as digging tools for clams and other mollusks. The bristly moustache is an important sensory organ. The yellowish-gray animal provides the Eskimos with meat, blubber, oil, building material for boats and shelter. The ivory tusks are a cash crop. Consequently, it is hunted and fished for with blubber as bait and its numbers have been steadily reduced. Its range is the Arctic Ocean, the open waters near the polar ice. In seasonal migrations most walruses travel south in winter, before the advance of the arctic ice, and north in spring. Instead of propelling themselves they prefer to ride on ice floes. Although the female walruses have four nipples only single calves are born to them.

A NEIGHBOR ON THE WATERFRONT. The seals we see occasionally sunning on rocks or playing in coves, from New Jersey northward on the Atlantic coast and from California northward on the Pacific shore, are harbor or hair seals. They are not confined to American waters but live in all oceans of the northern hemisphere. Their normal habitat is salt water and they are not migratory, but when a school of fish starts an upstream run in a river, the seals will follow it for several hundred miles. Male specimens have a length of about 6 feet; external ears are lacking. The color of their short, coarse fur varies from silvery to almost black, with grayish and brownish as intermediate shades; on the back they show darkish spots of various shades. Herring, cod and other fish are their daily food. In September, promiscuous mating takes place under water, in some secluded bay or cove; on selected spots ashore the single or twin pups are born, wrapped in a coat of soft, whitish wool which is shed soon after birth. These seals do not form harems but only loose colonies. They are friendly, inquisitive and intelligent, and can be tamed in a matter of hours; they become affectionate pets, strongly attached to their masters.

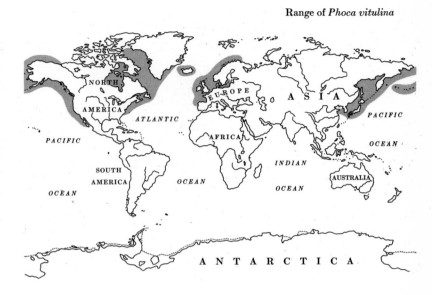

Range of *Phoca vitulina*

Harbor Seal

Phoca vitulina

Sea Elephant

Mirounga angustirostris

Range of
Mirounga angustirostris

A GROTESQUE GIANT. With a bull's length of up to 22 feet and a weight of approximately 3.5 metric tons, the sea elephant is the largest of the pinnipeds. Two species are known; the northern variety which is illustrated here inhabits our western coastal waters; it has been ruthlessly slaughtered and almost exterminated by commercial hunters but is now making a comeback. More numerous is the South Atlantic species whose range extends from Argentina to St. Helena and south. The animal's name refers to its 15-inch nose which looks like a miniature elephant's trunk; normally it flops over the mouth but when a bull wants to impress or frighten an attacker, he inflates the trunk and makes it swell until it stands almost straight up. Fish and cuttlefish are their principal food. For the mating season the animals congregate on land, on the beaches of offshore islands; there the big bulls rule their harems of 10 to 30 cows in extremely noisy rookeries; the male sea elephants produce trumpeting sounds while the females grunt and groan.

A Burrowing Ant-Bear

AARDVARK — TUBULIDENTATA

Except for the fact that the aardvark is one of the mammals it does not seem to have any relatives; therefore a special order, family and genus have been created for this single species. In the Afrikaans language the name means "earth pig," for it looks like a pig and seeks shelter and safety in the earth. Its exterior is grotesque; its long ears resemble those of a donkey and the aardvark moves them independently of each other and folds them back to keep them clean while burrowing. Its sticky tongue, about a foot long, often hangs out of its mouth, the end coiled like a pigtail. Its strength is prodigious; in one recorded instance three native adults tried to pull an aardvark out of its hole by the tail; they had to let go, and the aardvark won the tug of war.

A SHY BUT MIGHTY TERMITE-HUNTER. On the grassy plains and parklands of Africa south of the Sahara and the Sudan the aardvark spends its days in burrows which it digs with incredible speed. Its method is unique; while sitting on its hind legs and tail, its forefeet push the earth backward under its body in a steady stream of sand propelled 12 feet into the air. It actually digs itself into the ground, and its final structure is about 10 feet long, with an end chamber in which the animal can turn. Certain sections of Africa are honeycombed with aardvark holes, most of them abandoned, and thousands of other animals use them as shelter and nesting sites for their young. At night the aardvark cautiously emerges from its hole and wanders about for many miles in search of termites, ants and locusts. With its powerful claws it rips through the concrete structures of the African termites, opening up their brood galleries. Its thick hide is so impervious to insect bites that the aardvark sometimes falls asleep in a termite nest with thousands of insects clinging to its skin. The adult male's head-and-body length is approximately 5 feet, with a weight of 175 pounds. Its thick hide is covered with brownish or yellowish-gray hair which is darker on the legs.

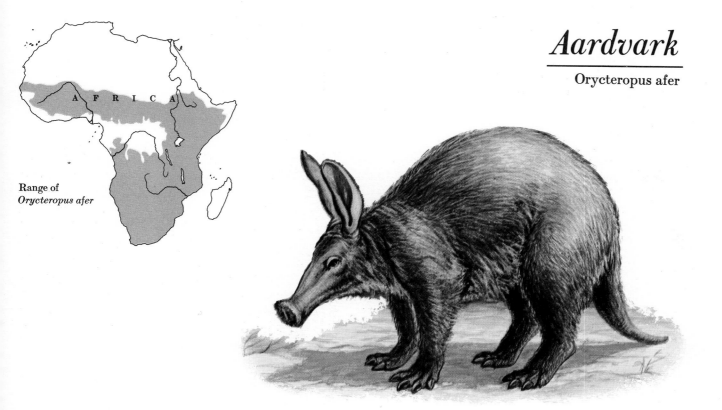

Range of
Orycteropus afer

Aardvark

Orycteropus afer

Versatile Noses

ELEPHANTS — PROBOSCIDEA

The most outstanding characteristic of the two living genera of this family is the trunk or proboscis, the flexible elongation of the nose with the nostrils at the end. The finger-like tip is a most sensitive tool; it serves equally well for picking up a berry as for testing the texture of a fruit or for probing the condition of the ground. The legs of these huge mammals are massive columns and in contrast to the structure of most quadrupeds their knees are located, like those of human beings, below their bodies. Their feet are short elastic pads with five toes; their bones are filled not with marrow but with a bony sponge. The tusks are ivory, the biggest specimen on record being 11 feet 5 inches long and weighing 293 pounds. The two genera consist of a single species each; the African elephant is the largest existing land animal while the Indian or Asiatic elephant occupies the third place, after the Indian rhino. Savannas, jungles and the valleys of lakes and rivers are their habitat. Since they consume huge amounts of forage — approximately 500 pounds per day — they have to be nomadic; some herds travel back and forth on a seasonal route within a year while others move in a circular course completing the cycle in longer periods. Baby elephants are born wth a "halo," a thin coat of brown hair which stands out from the skin. As they grow older, only few hairs remain and adults appear to be naked. Elephants are gregarious creatures living according to well established rules and customs; highly intelligent, they assist each other, particularly at the time of birth when several females act as the baby's nursemaids. The gestation period varies from 18 to 22 months and the baby is not weaned until it is five years old; it can expect to live for 70 to 80 years. Actually the family *Elephantidae* consists of eight genera; six, however, are extinct now, among them the well-known mammoth and mastodon. The former, covered with a coarse, woolly coat, inhabited the northern hemisphere and was hunted by early Stone Age man who drew the mammoth's picture on the walls of caves. Complete specimens with hide, hair, and tusks intact were discovered in the frozen ground of Siberia. The mastodon died out early in the Old World but survived in the western hemisphere into the days of the migrating tribes that traveled from Asia to the American continent; at various spots in the United States primitive weapons have been found in connection with mastodon bones. Both mammoths and mastodons had a shoulder height of about 10 feet, but while the former's tusks frequently showed a spiral form, those of the latter were straight and parallel. Both were vegetarians like today's elephants.

Indian Elephant

Elephas maximus

MAN AND BEAST IN CLOSE RAPPORT. While we usually associate the African elephant with freedom in the wilderness, we think of the Asiatic elephant as a helper of man, and as a worker in the teak yards of India; as a traditional symbol in ceremonial processions, and as a carrier of sportsmen at tiger hunts, or as a circus performer. Yet man's most spectacular employment of elephant power was conducted not with Indian but with African elephants when the Carthaginian general Hannibal used hordes of tamed beasts on his trek across the Alps against Rome. Occasionally African elephants have been beasts of burden in the Congo but these were exceptions. The Asiatic elephant, however, is part of the national life and folklore of India, Ceylon, Burma, Thailand, Malaya and Sumatra. There are certain castes in the jungles of Asia who have been elephant tamers for countless generations and have obtained an understanding of the animal's complex behavior that transcends scientific observation. Yet in spite of centuries of human association elephants have never been truly domesticated and rarely breed in captivity. But they assist in capturing young wild elephants in the jungle by gently calming down the prisoner's excitement and by escorting him to his new home. From the African species the Indian elephant is distinguished mainly by its smaller size, with a body length of up to 21 feet and a weight of about 5 metric tons, and its smaller ears. Its skin color, feeding habits and habitat are similar to those of its African relative. The Asiatic elephant is gregarious and travels in herds of 20 to 30 animals.

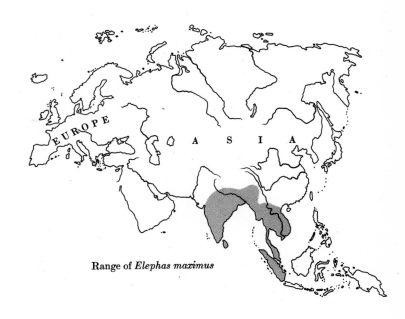

Range of *Elephas maximus*

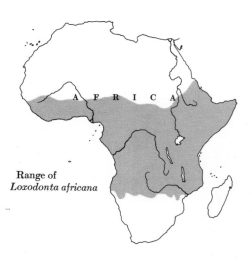

Range of
Loxodonta africana

THE LARGEST LAND ANIMAL ALIVE. With a body length of up to 25 feet and a weight of 8½ tons this huge animal has the power to uproot trees and trample its enemies to death. But it possesses also a uniquely delicate tool: the trunk. This projection of the nose with the nostrils at the end has a finger-like "lip" above and below, capable of picking up objects as small as a pea. The tubular trunk is also used as a water hose; it sucks up the liquid and sprays it into the elephant's mouth to quench its thirst, or over its back for a shower bath. The skin color is brownish-gray but since the animals like to roll on the ground and throw mud and dirt over their bodies, they assume the color of the soil. For their tusks, the source of ivory, the elephants have been hunted for centuries, throughout central and south Africa. At present they are protected in large areas and are holding their own; they forage on grass, leaves and fruits over a variety of terrain, from jungle to desert-like shrublands.

African Elephant

Loxodonta africana

Little Cousin of Big Beasts

HYRAXES — HYRACOIDEA

These small animals resemble rabbits or guinea pigs but have so many individualistic traits that a special order has been created for them. They are closely related to the ungulates, and anatomically their standing is near the elephants. Interestingly some African natives have come to the same conclusions without the benefit of science; they call the hyraxes "little brothers of elephants." The order contains only one family, three genera and about ten species. In the Old Testament, in Deuteronomy, Psalms and Proverbs, the hyraxes are called conies; Hebrew law forbade the eating of them for while they chew cud, it was said, they do not have cloven hoofs. In fact, they do not chew cud but only move their jaws as if they do, and they certainly have cloven hoofs. Arabs and Africans have always eaten their meat which, however, is reported to be dry and tough.

Rock Hyrax

Heterohyrax brucei

Range of
Heterohyrax brucei

A SUPERB MOUNTAINEER. In rocky, mountainous territory, at heights of up to 12,500 feet, the hyrax clings to rock surfaces that are almost perpendicular. Its toes are tipped with tiny hoofs, and its footpads, always moist, adhere to the stone wall with the effect of vacuum cups. Besides the "biblical" species which lives in Syria, Israel, Sinai and Arabia, the bulk of the genus *Heterohyrax* inhabits Africa from Ethiopia and the Congo to southern Rhodesia and southwest Africa. These animals are gregarious and live in colonies that may shelter hundreds of individuals; playfully they chase each other letting out shrill screams; in the afternoon they like to lie on ledges sunning themselves, or roll in the mud. In an interplay of wariness

and curiosity they run and return when alarmed. Their senses of vision and hearing are keen. If they are annoyed they attack and bite aggressively. Roots and bulbs which they gather in the early morning and late afternoon are their principal food; they also like locusts. The head-and-body length of a male adult is approximately 15 inches, with a weight of 10 pounds. The coat consists of thick, short hair in which the colors brown, white and black are intermingled. The underpart of the coat is white. In a fur-lined nest three young are born in March; on the very day of their birth they are able to romp and play with other youngsters. The life-span of the hyrax is estimated to be seven years.

Sirens of the Sea

SEA COWS — SIRENIA

Eight hundred years before Christ, Homer reported the fantastic tale of Odysseus' encounter with singing sirens who lived in the sea. In the era of the Roman Empire Pliny told similar stories, and during the epoch of exploration and discovery the world heard more accounts of mermaids nursing their babies at the breast like human beings. Today it is generally supposed that this myth is based on sightings of members of the family *Dugongidae* (dugongs) and of the family *Trichechidae* (manatees). These are large aquatic mammals with two nipples at the female breast. The fact that in the clear waters of tropical bays such "sirens" can be seen in a reclining semi-upright position may have added to the mystery. The manatees are of special interest since they are encountered in the coastal waters of the southeastern United States.

Range of *Dugong dugon*

Dugong

Dugong dugon

THE SEA COW OF AFRICA, ASIA AND AUSTRALIA. The dugong is a harmless saltwater dweller with a wide range. It is encountered in the Red Sea and on the east coast of Africa, the Bay of Bengal, in the East Indies and the Philippines, off New Guinea and the northern Australian coast. With a length of up to 12 feet it may weigh about 665 pounds; its skin is grayish-brown and its forelimbs are shaped like flippers. Stiff hairs grow around its muzzle. At intervals of one to ten minutes it surfaces in order to breathe; it feeds on the marine algae and grasses which it finds in shallow water. The single young sometimes rides on the back of its mother. The dugong is widely hunted, for its blubber yields a fine oil and its meat is generally appreciated; the natives of Madagascar consider it a prime delicacy. They also use the tallow for laxative purposes and use other parts of the dugong's body to cure various ailments. Once abundant, the dugong has been hunted to a point where its extermination is feared unless protective measures are taken.

North American Manatee

Trichechus manatus

THE SEA COW OF AMERICA. This dull-gray, inoffensive animal with a length of up to 14 feet and a weight
of about 1,500 pounds is distinguished by a number of interesting peculiarities. While almost all other mammals
have seven neck vertebrae, the manatee has only six; no
external ears exist; the upper lip is divided and each half-
lip moves independently of the other; the adult manatee
likes to rest on the surface in a marine bay or slow-flowing
river, with its back arched, holding its tail under its head;
if it touches ground, it "walks" on the tips of its flippers;
when young it swims with its flippers and when adult with
its tail; if stranded on land, it is immobilized and helpless.
In the Botanical Gardens of Georgetown, Guyana, several
tamed specimens have learned to perform simple tricks and
with their lips take food from the visitors' fingers. In
Guyana manatees are also employed in clearing waterways
of weeds which they do efficiently, feeding on plants that
thrive in saltwater, freshwater or brackish water. The northern species which is illustrated here ranges from the southeastern United States to Texas and the West Indies; it is
also encountered from Veracruz in Mexico to northern
South America; another species inhabits the regions of the
Amazon and the Orinoco, and a third is found in West
Africa. Since the meat, oil and hide of the manatee are of
excellent quality, it has been widely hunted and in certain
areas has become quite rare; in Florida it is legally protected.

Range of
Trichechus manatus

Hoofed Mammals

ODD-TOED UNGULATES — PERISSODACTYLA

Of the three living families of the odd-toed ungulates the horses-asses and the rhinos are natives of the Old World and live on grasslands and other types of open country. The tapirs are the only New World family of the order; their range extends from southern Mexico to Argentina where they inhabit forests and jungles. The special shape of the foot — one toe in the form of a hoof — enables these animals, particularly the horse, to be fast and enduring runners. They feed on plants as browsers and grazers. The domestication of the horse and the ass had a strong impact on the development of man and his way of life. In past geological ages the horse family had been far more numerous than it is now; it inhabited every continent except Australia. In America early smaller forms of the horse occurred but they died out and the American Indians had no knowledge of them. The first modern horses were brought to the New World by Cortez, in 1519. Spanish runaway horses multiplied in the American plains and turned the Plains Indians into expert horsemen. A few descendants of those feral horses survive as wild mustangs to this day.

EVEN-TOED UNGULATES — ARTIODACTYLA

The even-toed ungulates are probably the best-known and most useful of all orders of mammals. Many of their species have been domesticated and have helped man to multiply; his original hunting provided only limited supplies but the domesticated ungulates made possible the expansion of the human population and the creation of a civilization by furnishing huge amounts of food and clothing. The number of even-toed hoofed mammals in the service of man is large and includes not only the pig and the various breeds of domesticated cattle, the goats and sheep, but also the camel, the yak, the water buffalo, the llama, and the reindeer. The Mayas and Aztecs kept large herds of deer in corrals as meat providers. The order *Artiodactyla* has native representatives everywhere on our planet except in Australia and New Zealand. Smallest member of the order is the two-foot-long mouse deer, and the largest species is the hippopotamus, which may weigh 5 tons. With some minor exceptions they all possess an even number of digits; the two-toed foot is called a "cloven hoof." The pigs, peccaries and hippos have two- or three-chambered stomachs and do not ruminate. All others have three or four stomach chambers and are ruminants or cud-chewers. They feed on large amounts of vegetable food of low nutritional value and swallow it rapidly while no danger threatens. Then these ungulates rest at a safe, secluded place where the food is regurgitated into their mouths, mixed with additional saliva, chewed again and swallowed a second time.

Asiatic Wild Horse

Equus przewalskii

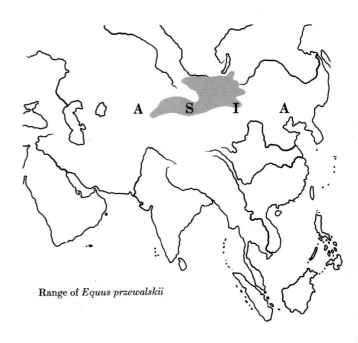

Range of *Equus przewalskii*

THE ONLY SURVIVING WILD HORSE. On the wide-open grasslands of the Mongolian plateau, in the region of the Altay Mountains, remnants of the only true wild horse survive. At one time the herds were huge, but in spite of the animals' wariness which keeps them out of man's sight, their numbers have been reduced by the natives almost to the point of extinction. Another danger is their loss of purity as a wild species; for occasionally they are joined by and bred with domesticated runaway ponies of the Mongolian natives. The horse was named for Nicolai Przewalski, a Russian army officer and explorer of the 19th century, who described the species scientifically. It is considered to be one of the ancestors of the domesticated horse. While the latter has developed toward long legs, a slender head, and a graceful body, the wild horse is small, stocky, and short-legged; its mane is erect and a forelock is absent. Its head-and-body length is approximately 6 feet, with a shoulder height of only 3½ feet and a weight of about 770 pounds. The smooth and short summer fur is reddish-brown above and yellowish-white below; the longer winter fur has lighter shades. The mane is dark brown, and a brown stripe runs along the back. Its life span is estimated at 25 to 30 years.

Zebra

Equus burchelli

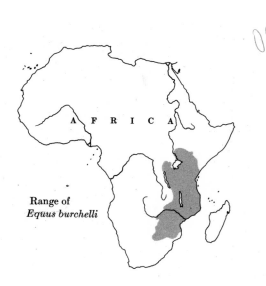

Range of
Equus burchelli

BEAUTIFUL BUT UNTAMABLE. A herd of zebras galloping over the grasslands of central, eastern or southern Africa is one of the world's most picturesque sights. The animals look strong, alert, well fed, and thoroughly at home in their environment when they mingle with groups of wildebeests, herds of gazelles, or flocks of ostriches. With their skin pattern of variously arranged dark stripes they are so conspicuous on a background of green vegetation that their design seems to be the opposite of mimicry; but in tall grass the vertical stripes make them almost invisible. Of the three species — distinguished by size, arrangement of bands, and other features — the common zebra is pictured here. It has a head-and-body length of up to 7 feet with a shoulder height of 4½ feet and a weight of 775 pounds. Its mane is erect, and the tail ends in a tuft of hair; no two individuals have the same pattern of bands. It is a speedy runner and has been clocked at 40 miles per hour; it is both inquisitive and shy but defends itself vigorously by kicking and biting; yet it is an easy prey for the lion who prefers zebra meat for his meals. In the African environment the zebra is far more disease-resistant than the horse and, therefore, attempts have been made to domesticate it; but it stubbornly resists all attempts to harness it to a cart, to use it as a riding animal, or to teach it any circus tricks. Experimentally it has been bred with both horses and asses, but again the results have not been encouraging. However, it adapts readily to captivity, is represented in every zoological garden, and may live to the age of 28 years.

A STURDY WILD ASS. Asses do not have an enviable reputation but in many ways they are admirable beasts; they are tough and patient, persevering and sure-footed. They stay healthy on very little food, and the wild species hardly need any water. The original range of the asses extends from Mongolia and Tibet in the east to Syria in the west, and throughout northern and eastern Africa. Plains with a semi-desert vegetation are their favorite habitat. The onager is one of the well-known species of asses; it roams over the shrublands of Iran, Afghanistan and northern India. Its head-and-body length is about 6 feet, its shoulder height approximately 5 feet, and its weight up to 570 pounds. The summer fur is reddish-brown; for the winter the coat gets denser and shaggier and changes to a lighter grayish shade. The mane is erect and coarse and the tail terminates with a bunch of hair. Onagers are encountered singly or in herds which, however, disperse when foaling time approaches. They are well-equipped for rapidly covering long distances, a necessity in a desert setting where food is scarce; this also explains the wide dispersal of the species.

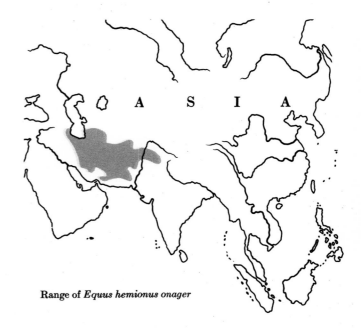

Range of *Equus hemionus onager*

Onager

Equus hemionus onager

Range of *Equus hemionus kiang*

THE COMMON ASS OF THE TIBETAN UPLANDS.
In herds of up to 100 individuals this wild ass of Tibet roams the arid tablelands, high up in the Himalaya. Its appearance is similar to that of the onager although it is somewhat larger. Its summer coat is reddish and white, its winter coat shaggy brown; its big hoofs are conspicuous. The herds break up at the beginning of foaling time, the young are born approximately 12 months later. Besides the wild asses, domesticated strains have been in existence since prehistoric times and are used as beasts of burden and riding animals. Usually called donkeys or burros, they still play an important part in areas where horses do not prosper; in underdeveloped countries where the people cannot afford the upkeep of horses; and in difficult and arid terrain where only a burro survives. In America's western and southwestern mountains the prospectors for precious metals always employed burros to carry their supplies. The "wild" donkeys encountered in the West are the descendants of runaway animals. Pictured here is the wild form, the kiang.

Kiang

Equus hemionus kiang

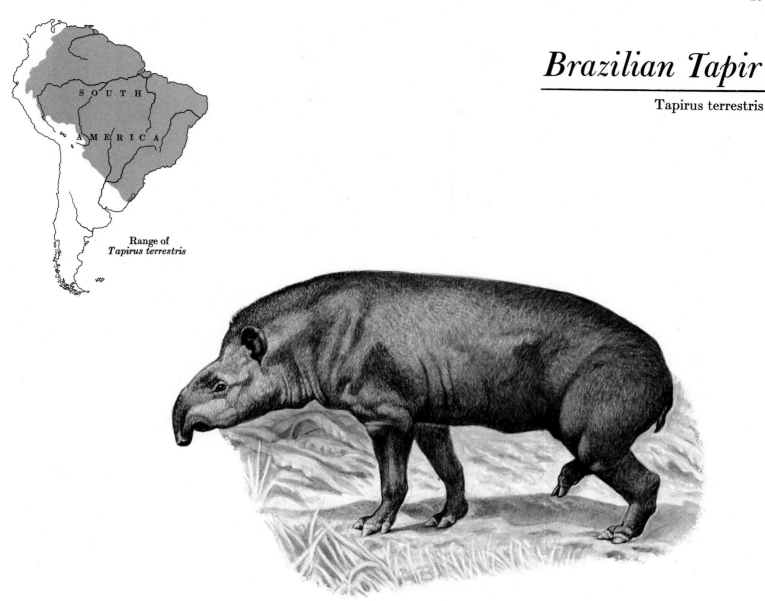

Range of
Tapirus terrestris

Brazilian Tapir

Tapirus terrestris

THE TAPIR'S CONTOUR TRAIL IN THE WILDERNESS. In the grassy or wooded habitat of these rather common South American mammals one element is essential: rivers or lakes with a constant water supply must be near. To reach these bodies of water the tapirs create trails which adapt themselves to the contours of the terrain so well that in some cases today's engineers have laid out and constructed modern mountain roads along the ancient tapir trails. The range of the Brazilian tapir extends from Venezuela and Colombia through South America to the Brazilian state of Rio Grande do Sul and the Gran Chaco region of Paraguay. Two other species are found nearby, one in the northwestern Andes Mountains, and one in Mexico and Central America. The fact that a fourth range of tapirs is located far away in Southeast Asia suggests that at one time the family inhabited an enormous territory extending over two continents, including the land bridge which at a fairly recent geological time connected America with Asia. Fossils found in the intervening regions seem to confirm the theory that the present-day tapirs are the survivors of an originally far larger group. An adult male Brazilian tapir may attain a length of up to 8 feet but many individuals are smaller. In contrast to the Malayan tapir the South American species has a low, narrow mane; the skin is dark brown but lighter below. The proboscis, a fleshy extension of snout and upper lip, is longer in the South American than in the Malayan species. In their environment tapirs are agile creatures; they run and climb, swim and dive skillfully. They are inoffensive and in case of danger dash into the water or the dense forest, but they also defend themselves by biting. They feed on both aquatic and terrestrial vegetation. Their principal enemy is the jaguar; sportsmen hunt them and natives kill them for their good meat although some Indian tribes consider them sacred and spare them. The name *tapir* is a word of the Tupí Indian language of Brazil.

Malayan Tapir

Tapirus indicus

Range of
Tapirus indicus

STRAIGHT ACROSS THE JUNGLE. This animal is perfectly constructed for charging through dense thickets. Its back is rounded and the front of its body tapers downward; the proboscis, a combination of nose and upper lip with nostrils at the tip, is usually held close to the ground, the best position for jungle travel. The skin is very thick, with a scattering of bristly hair. A most unusual feature is the white blanket that seems to be thrown over the blackish body; it may be a kind of mimicry. Tapirs grazing among gray boulders in a bright light are hard to distinguish. The largest specimens have a head-and-body length of 8 feet, with a shoulder height of 3¼ feet and a weight of about 660 pounds. They live in forests or grasslands where permanent streams and lakes are near. Alone or in pairs, they like to sleep in thickets at the shore by day and feed on aquatic plants at night, swimming and wading, splashing in the water and rolling in the mud. They are not confined to Malaya, as the name suggests, but are encountered also in Burma and Thailand, Indochina and Sumatra. They are shy and seek safety in flight but defend themselves by sharp bites when cornered; however, they are an easy prey for the tiger. The single young is born with a colorful design of white and yellow stripes and spots on a black background, but this coloration is lost after approximately half a year; the tapir may live to an age of 30 years.

VICTIM OF THE WITCH DOCTORS. This powerful beast with a body length of up to 13½ feet and a weight of about 4 metric tons has always been an object of awe and superstition. For centuries oriental despots had their drinking cups made of the horn of the Indian rhino because the magic horn was supposed to turn ineffective any poison that might have been added to the drink. In China the powdered horn is believed to be a strong aphrodisiac, and the customary price is half the horn's weight in gold. Also the rhino's dried blood is sold as a curative at high prices. These superstitions had tragic consequences for the species. Hunted ruthlessly for the practitioners of folk medicine, the rhino has disappeared from large areas in southeast Asia and is now confined to Nepal and northeast India. Its extraordinary appearance probably contributes to the folk tales of its mystical powers. Its elephant-like hide with its deep folds, pleats and bosses resembles medieval armor plate. The horn, about 2 feet long, is really a bunch of congealed hair, not connected with the bone structure; fringes of stiff hair adorn the ears and the tip of the tail. The animal looks ferocious but is harmless and shy; in fact, it survives only because it avoids human contacts and retires to inaccessible haunts, preferably to swampy jungle areas where it feeds on reeds and bathes daily. It is known to charge only when wounded or when defending a calf; in that case the female uses her sharp tusks for the attack, not her horn. A single young is born after a gestation period of 19 months; its life span is about 50 years.

Range of
Rhinoceros unicornis

Indian Rhinoceros

Rhinoceros unicornis

African Black Rhinoceros

Diceros bicornis

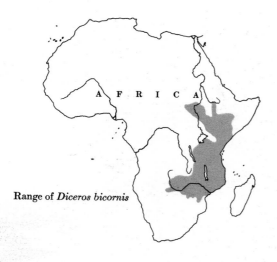

Range of *Diceros bicornis*

PLACID BUT NOT PREDICTABLE. In the great African national parks tourists take pictures of black rhinos without apprehension, but caution is advised. These powerful and somewhat dull beasts may become annoyed not only by what they see — their vision is quite poor — but by what they smell and hear so they may unpredictably charge a sound or an odor and crash through brush and forests in blind fury. They are reported to have overturned automobiles and to have impaled human beings on their front horns, throwing them high into the air. The range of these clumsy-looking but agile animals extends south from a line between Lake Chad and Ethiopia, through Central, East and South Africa. Each male rhino maintains for his family a defended territory which he marks with heaps of dung, spots where he urinates regularly, and sticks for body rubs which retain the owner's scent. The head-and-body length of a male adult is about 12 feet, with a weight of up to 2 tons. The color of the naked skin is dark brown rather than black. The larger but rarer white rhino is slate gray but not white. Here the word "white" is a mistranslation of the Dutch word "weit," meaning "wide"; it refers to the wide, squarish lips of that species.

ANCESTOR OF THE DOMESTIC PIG. The wild boar is a native of the Old World, with an enormous range that stretches from Europe through northern Africa and most of Asia to the East Indies. During the 19th century hunting clubs in the United States introduced it to the southern mountains where it has become established. The exact number of species has not yet been determined; there may be five or more. All, however, have a similar way of life; they are quick runners, strong swimmers, and devoted mud-wallowers. They have a curious way of improvising a green blanket by cutting grass, spreading it on top of tall, standing grass, and crawling under it. The head-and-body length of a male adult will be about 6 feet, with a weight of 440 pounds. The scant, bristly fur covering is brown, gray or black. Quite a few boars are adorned with side-whiskers and a mane. Two tusks in each jaw are a characteristic feature. In herds of 6 to 50 individuals they travel about while foraging for nuts and grains, roots and plants; insect larvae and carrion are also welcome. The 3 to 12 young in a litter are raised by the mother only. If left alone wild boars are harmless, but when alarmed they become very dangerous; boar hunts have been the sport of kings for centuries.

Range of *Sus scrofa*

Wild Boar

Sus scrofa

A GROTESQUE PIG. This common African animal is quite inoffensive but it looks ferocious. Big tusks, up to 2 feet long on an adult, protrude from the tip of the snout; long thin hair and rough bristles cover the blackish-brown body; ugly warts grow on the sides of the head and below the eyes; when it runs, the thin tail with the tuft at the end stands erect like a flagpole; when it feeds it comes down on its padded knees and shuffles along in that posture while eating and grunting. The curved tusks are used for digging up roots but also as a weapon; when the wart hog is cornered or defends its young it can inflict dangerous injuries. A grown-up male has a head-and-body length of up to 3½ feet, with a weight of approximately 220 pounds. Alone or in family parties these wild pigs roam the grasslands and light forests of Africa, mostly in the eastern and southern sections. During the day they feed on grass and berries, roots and seeds, bark and sometimes carrion; at night and during the hottest hours they rest in underground shelters which often are abandoned burrows of aardvarks. Like all members of the pig family they enjoy frequent mud baths. Sows bear litters of two to four with a life expectancy of up to 12½ years. Although lions, leopards and natives like the meat and kill many individuals, the species survives in large numbers.

Wart Hog

Phacochoerus aethiopicus

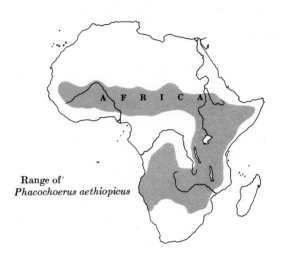

Range of
Phacochoerus aethiopicus

Collared Peccary

Tayassu tajacu

THE ONLY PIG-LIKE MAMMAL IN THE NEW WORLD. There are no true native pigs in America, but the peccaries are an approximation. Like pigs they are omnivorous and feed on tubers and cactus fruit, grubs and frogs, lizards and snakes; rattlesnake bites do not seem to affect them. Like pigs they also have a keen sense of smell and are able to detect a small bulb three inches underground before any shoots appear on the surface. When they get excited their hairs bristle and their dorsal glands exhale a musky odor which is noticeable yards away. As a warning of danger they noisily click their canine teeth. The range of the two species extends from Texas, New Mexico and Arizona, where they are sometimes called javelinas, southward to Patagonia. In bands of five to 15 they wander about, and since they do not follow a leader, it is supposed that their scent acts as a coordinating force. Speedily they take care of their enemies, of dogs, coyotes, and bobcats; if one of the band is pursued or injured the whole herd attacks the intruder. An adult male will attain a head-and-body length of up to 3¼ feet and a weight of up to 65 pounds. The color of the body is dark gray, with a whitish neck collar.

Range of
Tayassu tajacu

Hippopotamus

Hippopotamus amphibius

Range of
Hippopotamus amphibius

THE RIVER HORSE. The Greek word *hippopotamus* means "river horse," and rivers are indeed the principal habitat of the species; but they also dwell in lakes and pools. The hippo's range extends through Africa south of 17° north latitude. These waterbound terrestrial mammals spend most of the day in the water, their huge, barrel-like bodies submerged except for their eyes and nostrils. They mate in the water and give birth to young which can swim before they can walk. But at night all hippos emerge and wander overland, often for miles, feeding on grass and other vegetation and occasionally trampling down plantations and gardens. The hippo's weight is approximately 5 tons, with a head-and-body length of 15 feet; its most conspicuous part is its monstrous mouth; when at mating time two bulls challenge each other and make threatening moves, their wide-open jaws are a sight to behold. Their bite is powerful and they are able to scuttle a canoe but normally are phlegmatic and harmless. Hippos are still common on the rivers and lakes of tropical Africa — the prime source of meat for many native tribes.

DESIGNED FOR DESERT TRAVEL. The single-humped camel is no longer encountered in a wild state. Domesticated eons ago in Arabia, its range has expanded not only in the Near East and Africa but also as far as India and Australia. For thousands of years it has been the classical beast of burden of the desert, carrying loads of up to 600 pounds at the rate of 30 miles per day. For this task it is superbly equipped, with undivided soles on its feet and thick knee pads, heavy eyelashes and slit-like nostrils that can be closed in dust- and sand-storms. For days it may go without water, and if fresh water is not available it will drink seawater. If in an emergency none of the semi-desert vegetation on which it normally feeds is obtainable it will eat meat, bones, and even fish. To its owner it contributes flesh, hide, and sinews; from its droppings and urine chemicals are extracted, and its fermented milk is turned into an alcoholic drink.

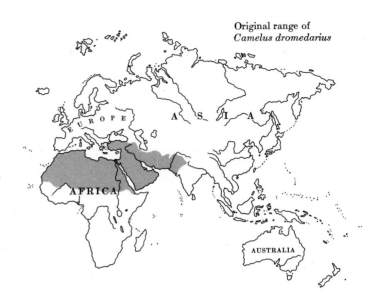

Original range of
Camelus dromedarius

Dromedary

Camelus dromedarius

THE COLD CLIMATE VERSION OF THE CAMEL. Wild bands of two-humped camels roam the plains of Central Asia, Sinkiang and Mongolia; during the summer they frequent the river valleys of the Gobi steppe but retreat to the desert for the winter. Their brown cold-weather coat consists of dense wool about two inches long, with bunches of thick, long hair hanging from head and neck, thighs and tail. These masses of wool are suddenly shed when summer arrives, leaving the animal shaggy and ragged-looking. There are also large herds of domestic two-humped camels; as beasts of burden they carry large loads at a speed of approximately ten miles per hour, plodding steadily even through winter blizzards. As riding animals they are easier to handle than their one-humped relatives. They eat anything that grows in arid soil, including salty plants that are strictly avoided by other grazing animals. For long periods they can go without water, but since they have no way of storing it within their bodies, they have to drink deeply from time to time; about 14 gallons will restore the body moisture they need; while they prefer fresh water they will also drink brackish or even salt water. An adult male will have a head-and-body length of up to 10 feet, with a weight of 1,530 pounds. The two humps of this camel will stand erect, firm and bulbous, if it is well fed; otherwise they will shrink and lean sideways.

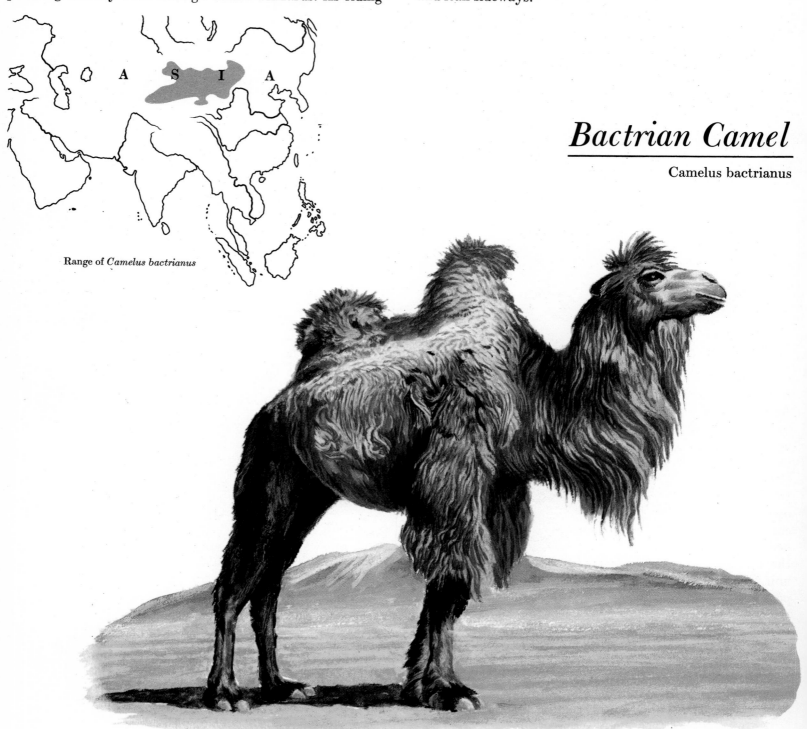

Range of *Camelus bactrianus*

Bactrian Camel

Camelus bactrianus

Guanaco

Lama guanacoe

WILD LLAMA OF THE HIGH PAMPAS. On the Andean mountain plateaus of southern and western South America small herds of guanacos can be seen grazing or resting, lying down in their characteristic way: They drop on their front knees, then on their hindquarters, and come to rest with their legs tucked under their bellies. They also like to wade and stand in mountain streams, letting the water rush around their bodies. Clearly visible on the open high pampas, they have to be shy and alert, and in case of danger dash off at a speed of up to 35 miles per hour. Each band consists of four to ten females under the leadership of a male; they form an unusually loyal unit. If the leader is killed the females do not rush off in panic but congregate around the carcass, nudge it, try to help their master and to restore him to life. Males fight each other occasionally, letting out screams of high and growls of low pitch. An adult has a head-and-body length of approximately 6 feet, with a shoulder height of 3 feet and a weight of about 210 pounds. Its coat is brown with white underparts and a gray-black face. The female has four teats, but only a single young is born every other year; it is able to run vigorously on its birthday.

Range of *Lama guanacoe*

THE ONLY BEAST OF BURDEN DOMESTICATED BY THE NATIVE PEOPLES OF THE AMERICAS. When the Spaniards conquered the Inca Empire, they discovered that hundreds of thousands of llamas were the living basis of the native culture. These beasts lugged loads for thousands of miles up and down the country, on roads especially built for them, worked in the silver and gold mines and with a complicated system of knots tied into the fur of the animal's undersides carried government messages to the far corners of the realm. Even today the llamas are indispensable to the natives; at a height of 16,000 feet where no other animal is able to carry a burden they proceed at 16 miles per hour with loads of

210 pounds. Their meat, fresh or jerked, and their milk feed the Indians, their fleece clothes them, and their dried droppings burn to warm their huts. In addition, the hair of the animal is braided into ropes and their tallow is used to make candles. The head-and-body length of the llama is about 4 feet, and since it is a tall creature, its shoulder height is the same; its weight may reach 210 pounds. The coloration of the fine, thick woolly coat is a pattern of irregular brown, black and white blotches, but quite a few individuals show one of these colors only. The llama's habitat is the semi-desert bordering the high ranges of the Andes Mountains, and extends from about a 16,000-foot elevation to sea level.

Llama

Lama peruana

Range of *Lama peruana*

Alpaca

Lama pacos

THE WORLD'S CHAMPION WOOL-BEARER. The quantity of wool grown by an alpaca surpasses that of any other animal; like a blanket its coat hangs down almost to the ground. This close relative of the llama has been domesticated and bred for wool production for as long as the llama has been raised as a bearer of burdens. Also the quality of alpaca wool is outstanding; in pre-Spanish days it was woven into royal robes, and today a coat of alpaca hair commands the same price as a fine fur coat. In size the alpaca is somewhat smaller than the llama but its coloration is of a similar variety, red or brown, black or white. With the other members of the genus *Lama* it shares the habitat and the range as well as a number of peculiar habits. It spits when annoyed and sometimes adds a small stone to the saliva, for stronger effect. When running it lifts simultaneously the feet first on one side, then on the other, a gait which produces a graceful motion.

Range of *Lama pacos*

A FLEECE FOR INCA ROYALTY. The vicuña which is considered the most graceful of all hoofed animals has a pelt so fine, soft and silky that in pre-Spanish days it was reserved for the royal family of the Incas and their nobility; particularly valued was the fleece that at a certain season of the year hangs from the throat of males. The range of the vicuña extends from latitude 10° south along the Andes Mountains for more than 1,200 miles; the rolling plains at altitudes of 12,000 to 18,000 feet are its habitat. Grazing on the short perennial grasses, the vicuñas roam the tablelands in bands of five to 15 females led by a male who in case of danger will take a stand between the intruder and the fleeing females. Such a male may have a head-and-body length of 5 feet, with a shoulder height of 2 feet 10 inches and a weight of 144 pounds; the woolly coat is brown, with a white or yellowish "bib." Vicuñas have some interesting habits. Like the llamas they spit when angry, vigorously expelling a bit of saliva with air; they keep community dung piles for urinating and defecating; they like to roll on the ground to scratch their bodies. They are capable of running 30 miles per hour at an altitude of 15,000 feet. Various attempts to domesticate them have failed, and they are hunted for their meat and their wool. By law the animals are protected but the law is not enforced; wildlife experts feel that they would respond favorably to scientific conservation. A single young is born in February; it will have a life span of 15 to 20 years.

Vicuña

Vicugna vicugna

Range of *Vicugna vicugna*

European Red Deer

Cervus elaphus

Range of *Cervus elaphus*

EUROPE'S BEST-KNOWN GAME ANIMAL. The red deer is the principal target of European hunters; in many parts of the continent it is fed during the winter; bundles of hay are dropped in the forest, and the deer is actually half-tame. An adult buck is an animal of impressive size, with a head-and-body length of up to 8 feet and a weight of 550 pounds. Its coat is brownish-red with lighter underparts; the buttocks show a light patch, and in some strains a dark stripe runs along the back. These deer are far more gregarious than the American white-tailed deer; each herd stays in a circumscribed territory which they do not leave. In the fall the stags shed the velvet from their horns, and collect a harem for the mating season during which they express their mood with a deep, bellowing roar.

Range of
Odocoileus virginianus

THE BEST-LOVED NATIVE OF OUR AMERICAN FORESTS. From Canada through the United States to northern South America the white-tailed or Virginia deer can be observed feeding on grass and herbs, mushrooms and nuts, its reddish summer coat glowing in the afternoon sun. Gracefully it leaps over hurdles or dashes across a road. It is also part of our history. Early settlers ate venison, wore moccasins and buckskin breeches, and sometimes used the deer's winter coat as a life preserver; on account of its tubular hairs it floats. A grown buck will attain a head-and-body length of 6 feet, with a weight of 300 pounds. The reddish summer fur will turn brownish-gray in winter. The male antlers are shed in late winter and begin to grow again in spring. These deer are solitary or travel in small groups; in winter only they sometimes congregate in "yards" where feeding conditions are favorable. In spring one or two beautifully spotted fawns are born; in the wild the white-tailed deer have a life expectancy of about 10 years.

American White-tailed Deer

Odocoileus virginianus

Mule Deer

Odocoileus hemionus

THE BIG-EARED DEER OF THE WESTERN MOUNTAINS. The big ears are the only reason for the name "mule deer" which is paralleled by the Mexican-Spanish name *venado burro*. This relative of the Virginia deer lives in the craggy and rocky forest areas of the western mountains, from Alberta and Manitoba, through our states between the Pacific Ocean and the Great Plains, southward to the tablelands of Mexico. During the summer the mule deer can be seen browsing on the high mountain ridges where they have a free field of vision and where the strong winds keep the flies away, for their new velvet-covered antlers are sensitive to insect attacks. To negotiate the broken terrain on the mountain slopes they have developed a peculiar gait which they prefer to running: With their four feet they spring from the ground in a kind of broad jump, and in jerky bounds travel up and down the hillsides. Measurements and coloration are similar to those of the white-tailed deer; but mule deer are heavier and have a black-tipped tail.

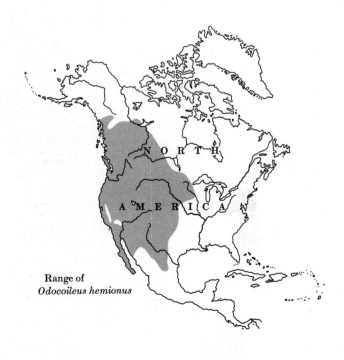

Range of
Odocoileus hemionus

Range of *Alces alces*

GIANT OF THE NORTH WOODS. This largest member of the deer family has an impressive appearance; an adult bull may attain a head-and-body length of 10 feet, with huge, scoop-like antlers spreading for 6 feet. In spite of its bulk — it may weigh as much as 1,800 pounds — it travels through the dense woods with ease, browsing on trees and bushes. In lakes it can be seen almost entirely submerged, feeding on succulent plants and roots at the bottom. Moist forests are its habitat, in its range which in the New World encompasses Alaska, Canada, and certain sections of the northern United States; in Europe it is encountered in Scandinavia and Russia, and in Asia in Siberia, Manchuria and Mongolia. Its summer coat is dark grayish-brown with lighter underparts, its winter fur is gray. A skin flap called "bell" hangs under the throat. The single young follows its mother for two years.

Moose

Alces alces

Caribou or Reindeer

Rangifer tarandus

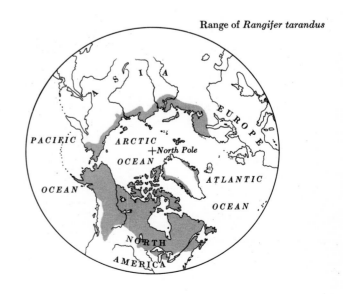

Range of *Rangifer tarandus*

THE DEER OF THE ARCTIC. This species is known in the New World as caribou, in the Old World as reindeer. The caribou has never been tamed; the reindeer is smaller, and while some wild herds are still reported to exist, it has been semi-domesticated for untold centuries by the Lapps who until recently derived from it all their food and clothing needs; they also use reindeer as riding and draft animals. In America the caribou used to gather, each fall, in herds of hundreds of thousands, to wander from the open tundra to forested areas; today their numbers are greatly reduced. Head and body of the species may measure 7 feet, with a weight of up to 700 pounds. Both sexes carry sweeping antlers. They are well-prepared for their environment, with a brownish-grayish, woolly undercoat and straight guard hairs for warmth and broad hoofs for walking on snow.

A TWENTIETH CENTURY DISCOVERY. It seems strange that a conspicuous mammal as big as an ox, quite common in its range and hunted and eaten by native pygmy tribes for centuries, should have been unknown to the civilized world until 1900; but it happened. The reasons were environmental: okapis live in the damp, often impenetrable rain forests of the eastern Congo, an area long avoided by white men; besides, okapis are suspicious, vigilant and wary to the point of fleeing into the dense jungle at the slightest alarm. The okapi's head-and-body length is about 6½ feet, with a weight of approximately 465 pounds. Its sleek coat looks maroon, with a purplish-reddish tinge; the color of the face is lighter; black and white stripes are conspicuous on buttocks and legs. Its tongue is so long that it is used for cleaning the ears. Only males carry small horns. Okapis are never encountered in herds but only singly or in small bands; they forage on leaves, fruits and seeds.

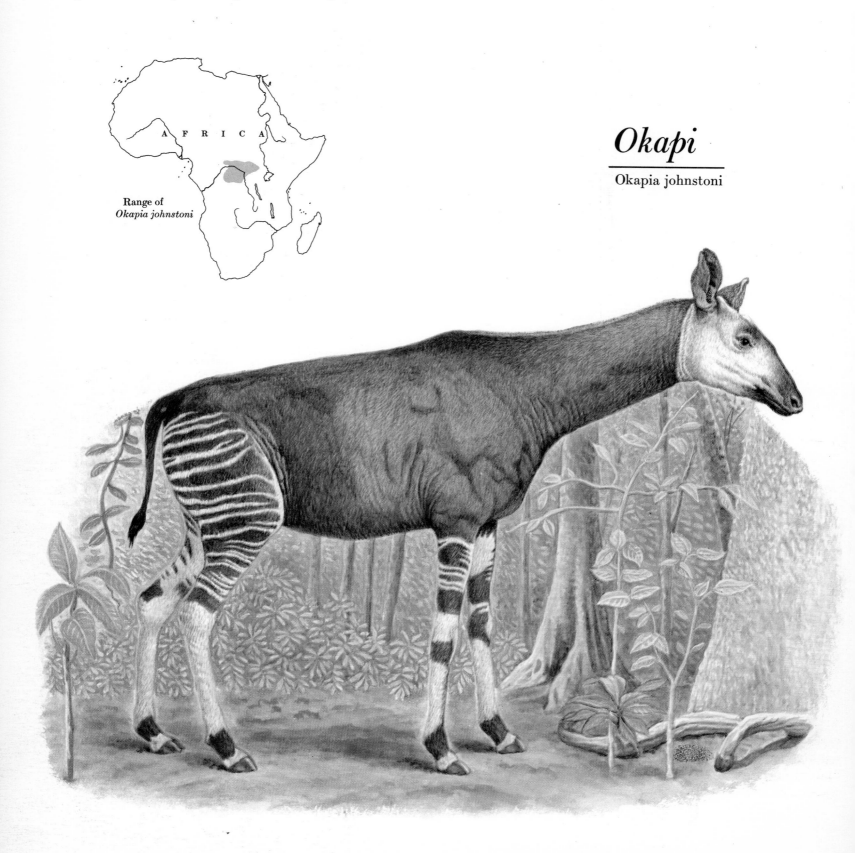

AFRICA

Range of
Okapia johnstoni

Okapi
Okapia johnstoni

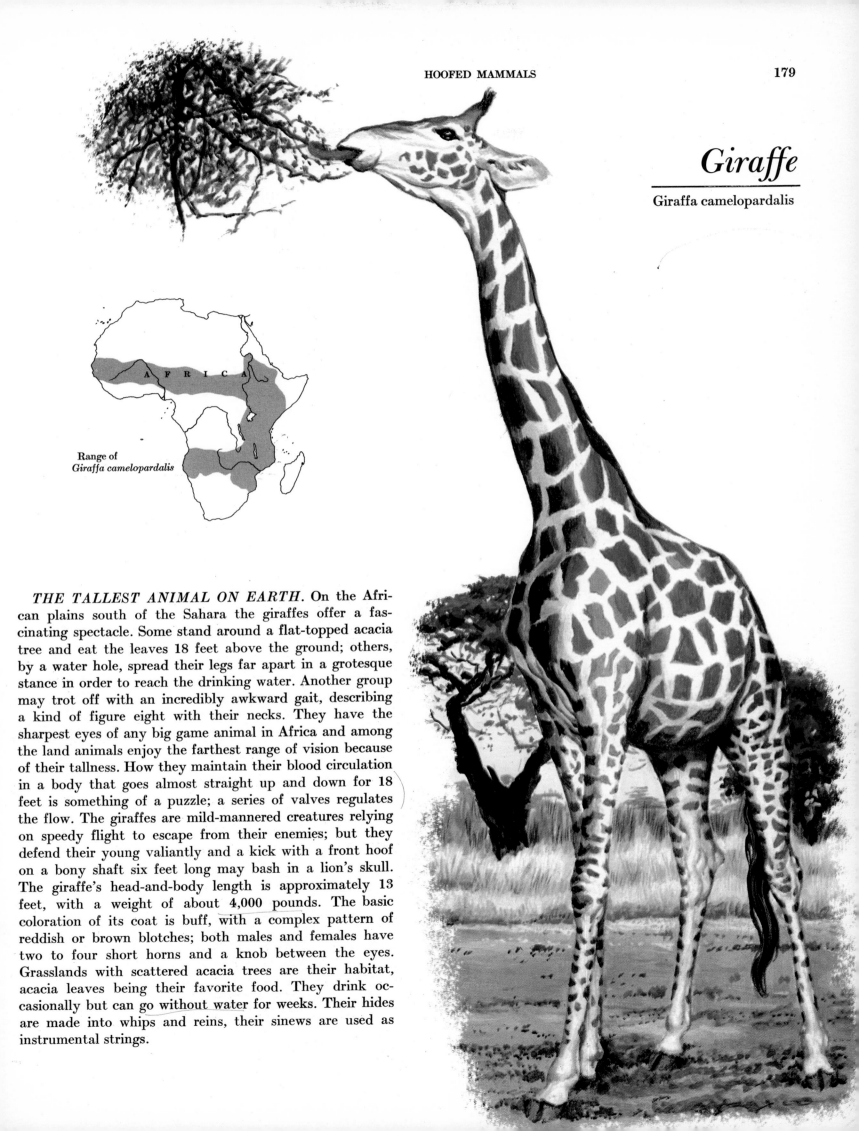

Giraffe

Giraffa camelopardalis

Range of
Giraffa camelopardalis

THE TALLEST ANIMAL ON EARTH. On the African plains south of the Sahara the giraffes offer a fascinating spectacle. Some stand around a flat-topped acacia tree and eat the leaves 18 feet above the ground; others, by a water hole, spread their legs far apart in a grotesque stance in order to reach the drinking water. Another group may trot off with an incredibly awkward gait, describing a kind of figure eight with their necks. They have the sharpest eyes of any big game animal in Africa and among the land animals enjoy the farthest range of vision because of their tallness. How they maintain their blood circulation in a body that goes almost straight up and down for 18 feet is something of a puzzle; a series of valves regulates the flow. The giraffes are mild-mannered creatures relying on speedy flight to escape from their enemies; but they defend their young valiantly and a kick with a front hoof on a bony shaft six feet long may bash in a lion's skull. The giraffe's head-and-body length is approximately 13 feet, with a weight of about 4,000 pounds. The basic coloration of its coat is buff, with a complex pattern of reddish or brown blotches; both males and females have two to four short horns and a knob between the eyes. Grasslands with scattered acacia trees are their habitat, acacia leaves being their favorite food. They drink occasionally but can go without water for weeks. Their hides are made into whips and reins, their sinews are used as instrumental strings.

Pronghorn Antelope

Antilocapra americana

Range of
Antilocapra americana

THE NEW WORLD'S FASTEST RUNNER. The pronghorn's capacity for swift motion begins early. At the age of four days it can outrun a human being. As an adult it travels at speeds of up to 42 miles per hour, with occasional leaps spanning up to 20 feet. Its cruising speed is slower, and after runs of three or four miles it usually has to take a break. This reddish-brown animal, not a true antelope, is a North American phenomenon. The bony core of its horns is permanent but the sheath which covers it, is shed every year after the breeding season. It has large and keen eyes which are able to distinguish objects miles away. It can erect the hair on its body when it wants to be cooled and turn it down for warmth. It raises its conspicuous white rump patch as a warning signal, and other pronghorns grazing as far as two and one half miles away will take notice. Its head-and-body length is about 5 feet, with a weight of 130 pounds; the females are smaller. Its range extends from the grasslands of southwestern Canada through the western United States to northern Mexico. During the summer pronghorns roam in small bands but converge in herds of 100 and more during the winter. One or two young are born in spring.

A WARY DWELLER OF THE TIMBERED MOUN-TAINS. It is not easy to encounter and approach these cautious animals which possess sharp ears and a wary disposition. By day they hide in inaccessible forest glens in rough and craggy hill and mountain country, and do their grazing and browsing only early in the morning and late in the evening. A few greater kudus have also been observed on plains with a thornbush vegetation. They are large beasts, second in size only to the eland, with a head-and-body length of 8 feet, a shoulder height of about 5 feet and a weight of 600 pounds. Their coat is reddish-to bluish-gray with thin white lines running down the rump. The males have huge horns which measure up to four feet along the curves and are a dangerous weapon during the rutting season. When two bulls fight, their horns sometimes become intertwined to such an extent that they cannot be separated, and both kudus die together. The range of the greater kudu extends over most of South Africa, south of a line from northern Angola in the west to Ethiopia in the east. Bulls roam in small bands of six to seven while females and young form herds of family groupings. They are good runners but have the habit of stopping frequently in order to look back; this custom has proved deadly to many of them. They are also outstanding jumpers; leaps of 30 feet have been observed, also jumps over eight-foot-high bushes, without damage to a twig.

Range of
Tragelaphus strepsiceros

Greater Kudu

Tragelaphus strepsiceros

Range of
Taurotragus oryx

A POTENTIAL DOMESTIC ANIMAL? Elands can be tamed, and some experts feel that they might be successfully domesticated, for their big, oxlike bodies offer tasty and tender meat in large quantities; their thick hides can be tanned into superior leather, and their long, spiraling horns are highly decorative. The excellent quality of the meat endangers the elands in the wild where lions and natives alike appreciate their flesh; besides, these animals are slow-moving and can be run down quite easily. On the other hand they possess keen senses and are wary and cautious; at the slightest sign of danger they dash off, probably in single file, with the bulls forming the rear guard. The eland may attain a head-and-body length of 11 feet and a weight of 2,000 pounds; its coat has a pale fawn color with whitish stripes around the upper section of the body. In their central and south African range elands roam the plains in herds of a few to more than 100 animals, feeding on foliage, fruits and bulbs; they can survive without drinking for months. A single young is born at no particular season.

Eland

Taurotragus oryx

Nïlgai

Boselaphus tragocamelus

NILGAIS AND SACRED COWS. On the Indian peninsula which is the range of this species, the Hindus consider the nilgai a near relative of the sacred Brahma cattle and therefore do not touch it. Consequently the nilgai does not show any fear in the presence of man and raids fruit orchards and sugarcane fields with impunity. Since its meat is not tasty to humans and its horns are too small to be a trophy, there is no incentive to hunt it. However, leopards and particularly tigers have a preference for nilgai meat and kill a great many of them. This largest native Indian antelope inhabits jungles and forests and is encountered only rarely on the plains. A male may reach a head-and-body length of 6½ feet, with a shoulder height of 5 feet and a weight of about 440 pounds. The dark-gray bull has short horns, various white markings and a black throat tuft; the coloration of the cows is somewhat lighter. The nilgais forelegs are longer than the hind legs. The males usually lead a solitary life while the females and young browse or graze in herds. Nilgais are easily tamed and breed readily in captivity.

Range of *Boselaphus tragocamelus*

Range of *Bubalus bubalis*

Water Buffalo

Bubalus bubalis

POWERFUL, SEMI-AQUATIC, TEMPERAMENTAL. This is one of the species which, like the yak, exist simultaneously in a tame and wild condition. For hundreds of years it has been domesticated from Egypt to India and the Philippines but wild herds are still reported from the moist jungles of Nepal, Bengal and Assam. Intermediate stages also occur, in the case of feral bands or when herds with human owners are confined so loosely that they are practically free. The name is derived from the fact that these animals like to stay submerged in water with only their nostrils protruding. They also love to wallow in wet dirt until they are caked with mud, a protection against insect pests. They have a temperamental disposition; although they are big and powerful with their 10-foot-long gray-black bodies and their formidable recurved horns, a small native boy whom they know well can easily guide them and even abuse them with impunity. These same beasts may attack, injure and kill a stranger who tries to take their picture. Docile beasts of burden of great strength, they have a pulling capacity far greater than that of regular draft oxen. The buffalo cows are milked regularly; buffalo meat is edible but tough, and the leather is of superior quality.

Zebu

Bos indicus

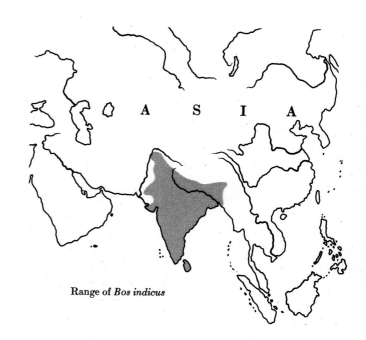

THE SACRED CATTLE OF INDIA. While no longer encountered in a wild stage, the zebu or Brahma cows enjoy the freedom of India, roam towns, villages and markets and help themselves to all the vegetable food they care to eat. For to the Hindus they are symbols of sustaining life, with a kind of mother image. The zebu is of approximately the same size as our domestic cattle but it has characteristic features: it is humped, has drooping ears and a big dewlap; its coloration may be cream, gray, or black. Some Brahma strains have been imported to semi-tropical America, and although they represent a different species they have been bred successfully with our native cattle, to create a heat-insect-and-disease-resisting type. The best-known hybrid is the Santa Gertrudis strain of the King Ranch in Texas.

Range of *Bos indicus*

THE OX OF THE HIMALAYA. This species thrives in the most desolate environment on the world's tallest mountains, at elevations of up to 20,000 feet. Well adapted to the cold, rocky waste, the yaks are strong and sure-footed, warmed by a coat of long, dense hair that hangs like a fringe around the body, down to the ankles; they do not prosper in a warmer climate. The wild bulls, usually congregating in groups of two or three, are big, brownish-black animals standing 6½ feet high at the shoulder; they carry large, upward-curving horns. The females and calves graze in big herds. In Tibet there is also a centuries-old strain of domesticated yaks; these tame beasts are considerably smaller and have coats of red, black, brown or particolored hair. They carry burdens, provide superior beef, and are milked regularly. A mixture of rich yak butter and tea is a popular Tibetan dish.

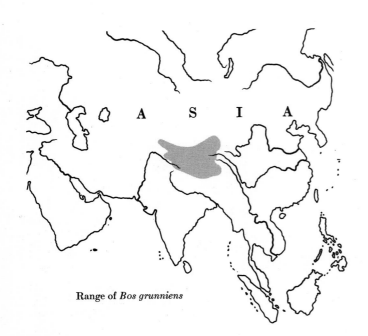

Range of *Bos grunniens*

Yak

Bos grunniens

Gaur

Bos gaurus

WILD CATTLE OF THE DEEP FOREST. A gaur bull is a huge brownish-black beast with white stockings, with a head-and-body length of 10 feet and a shoulder height of up to 7 feet; the females are only slightly smaller. Gaurs live in rocky hill country at altitudes ranging from 2,400 to 6,000 feet, and rarely leave the dense jungle for the open tablelands. The herds, consisting of five to 20 and usually eight to 12 animals, feed on grass, leaves, and sometimes on bark, in the morning and evening. Their range extends from central India eastward to Burma, Thailand, Indochina and the Malay Peninsula. Their productive cycle is adapted to the seasons; they mate during the dry part of the year and the calves are born in August and September. At that time the torrential monsoon rains have filled the streams with water and provided a new growth of tender grasses and herbs. During that period each herd occupies a well defined territory which is defended by the bull against intruders. When alarmed, the whole herd crashes through the jungle; the thundering noise can be heard far and wide. Their call is a combination of snort and whistle, but they also produce the typical "moo" sound of domestic cattle.

Range of *Bos gaurus*

Range of *Bos banteng*

TRUE WILD CATTLE. In herds of 10 to 30 individuals these wary and cautious forest dwellers spend the day resting in inaccessible thickets. At night they become active and feed hour after hour, interrupting their meal from time to time for cud-chewing. Their range originally extended from Burma eastward to Thailand, Indochina, the Malay Peninsula and Java. However, lately they have become very rare. Somewhat larger than our domestic cattle, an adult bull's head-and-body length may reach 6½ feet, with a shoulder height of 5 feet and a weight of 1,200 pounds. Occasionally solitary bulls of an even larger size are encountered. Their horns are shaped like those of the buffalo. The color of the bantengs has been described as blackish-brown with a bluish hue; white stockingfeet and a white patch on the rump are typical markings. During the dry months which are also the mating season they roam the valleys, preferring the open woods where they feed on grass; easy availability of water apparently is not essential. When the monsoons arrive, they wander into the hills and mountains, up to an altitude of 6,000 feet; there they enjoy the tender new vegetation, especially the succulent bamboo shoots. The single calf is born in August or September. A close relative of the banteng, the gaur (*Bos gaurus*) is a huge wild ox with the same white stockingfeet and a similar coloration. It lives in an area extending from central India to Indochina.

Banteng

Bos banteng

African Buffalo

Syncerus caffer

AFRICA'S MOST DANGEROUS BIG GAME ANIMAL. Watching a peacefully grazing herd of African buffaloes from a landrover or a launch on the Nile seems a harmless pastime. But in the open country great caution is advised. Old bulls will stalk and attack a human being even if not provoked. A hunter who has wounded a buffalo can be sure that the animal is lying in wait for him, ready for a deadly charge. As far as predatory animal foes are concerned, the buffaloes do not need to be alarmed; even a lion has only half a chance of success. These powerful beasts who inhabit Africa south of the Sahara have a head-and-body length of up to 10 feet and a shoulder height of 5 feet; bulls may weigh as many as 2,000 pounds. The young are covered with thick reddish- or blackish-brown hair; they lose much of it when they mature and are often hairless when old. The form is bulky, the chest broad, the strong horns are deadly. These buffaloes usually live in herds of 12 to several hundred, with an old female in the lead. In the morning and evening they drink, splash in the water and roll in the mud. During the heat of the day they rest, and they graze and browse in the early part of the night.

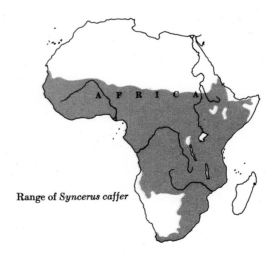

Range of *Syncerus caffer*

American Bison

Bison bison

Original range of *Bison bison*
• Present reserves of *Bison bison*

A MAGNIFICENT AMERICAN SPECIES. Fifty million bison — mistakenly called buffaloes — once roamed the North American continent, from the Great Slave Lake to Mexico. Huge herds migrated with the seasons, followed by grizzly bears and Indian tribes who depended on the bison for their livelihood. When the white man arrived the wanton slaughter began, and by 1889 only individuals that could be numbered in the hundreds were left alive. At that point conservationist forces went to work on the bison's resurgence, and now this splendid native species is safe for survival. Today's herds are protected although the reservations of the Canadian wood buffaloes, a subspecies, are so extensive that the animals live practically in the wild. An adult bull may have a length of up to 11½ feet, with a weight of 3,000 pounds. Long, shaggy brownish-black hair covers the front part of its body while the hair of the hind parts is lighter and shorter. Humped shoulders and short, sharp, powerful horns are characteristic for both males and females of the species.

A NEAR-EXTINCT RELATIVE OF THE AMER-ICAN BISON. In prehistoric times the European bison, also called wisent, occupied most of the European continent; but its fate was similar to that of the American species, and today only a few hundred specimens survive, mostly in zoological gardens. In the big, swampy Białystok Forest in eastern Poland a small wild herd may still be in existence. Measurements and weight are similar to those of the American bison but the wisent's hair is shorter and less copious, the horns are longer and less curved. Since it is plagued by parasites, it finds relief by rolling on the ground and scratching its body on tree trunks. While the American bison eats grass and prefers the prairies, the wisent rather inhabits open woods and browses on leaves, twigs, and bark. The gestation period is nine months, and the single calf follows its mother for three years; its life expectancy is approximately 20 years.

▨ Original range of *Bison bonasus*
● Present reserve of *Bison bonasus*

European Bison

Bison bonasus

A SPECTACULAR TROPHY. These big antelopes have an impressive appearance: they stand up to 7 feet high at their shoulders, their heads crowned with ringed horns rising straight up for another 3½ feet; seen in profile, they resemble the unicorn of the medieval legend. Their cream, brown or gray skin is adorned with dark markings which are pronounced in the face. The horned head is a much-sought trophy, and for that reason oryxes have been hunted extensively. In the Arabian desert a vicious type of chase with machine-gun fire from automobiles has practically exterminated the local species. In pre-colonial days the native warriors made shields of the strong and tough oryx hide and used the sharp points of the horns for their spears. The four species of the genus *Oryx* are distinguished geographically; the beisa or eastern African species is still quite frequent in certain areas of Kenya; the southern African variety or gemsbok inhabits the Kalahari desert; the scimitar-horned oryx lives in the Sahara and the Libyan deserts; and the Arabian species is almost extinct. The habitat of the genus varies from deserts to rocky hillsides and brushwoods where the wary and alert animals roam in bands of two to 12; occasionally herds of up to 60 individuals have been observed. When cornered or injured they lower their sharp horns and ram them into the enemy; such an attack may be fatal even to a lion. Pictured here is the gemsbok of South Africa.

Gemsbok

Oryx gazella

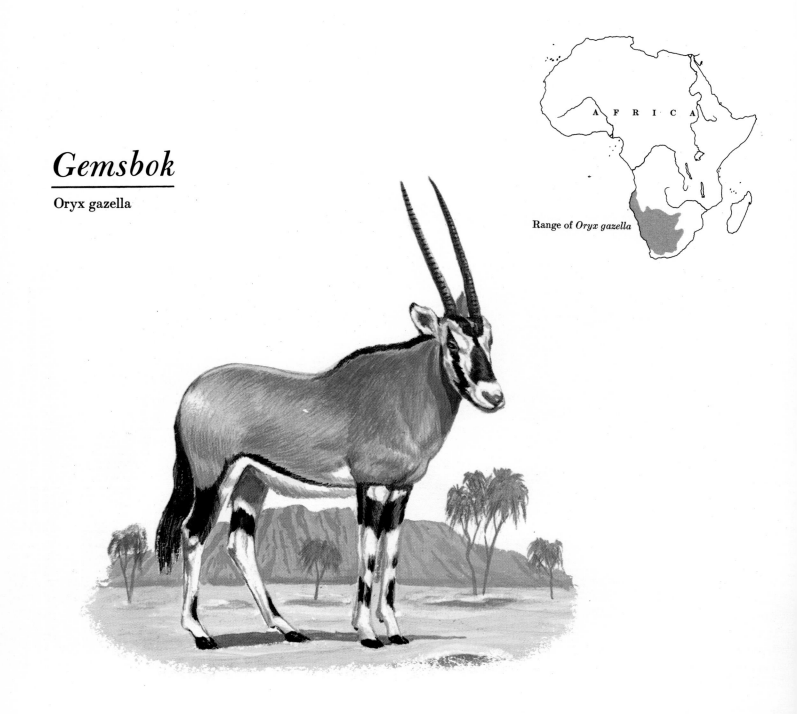

AFRICA

Range of *Oryx gazella*

Red Hartebeest

Alcelaphus buselaphus

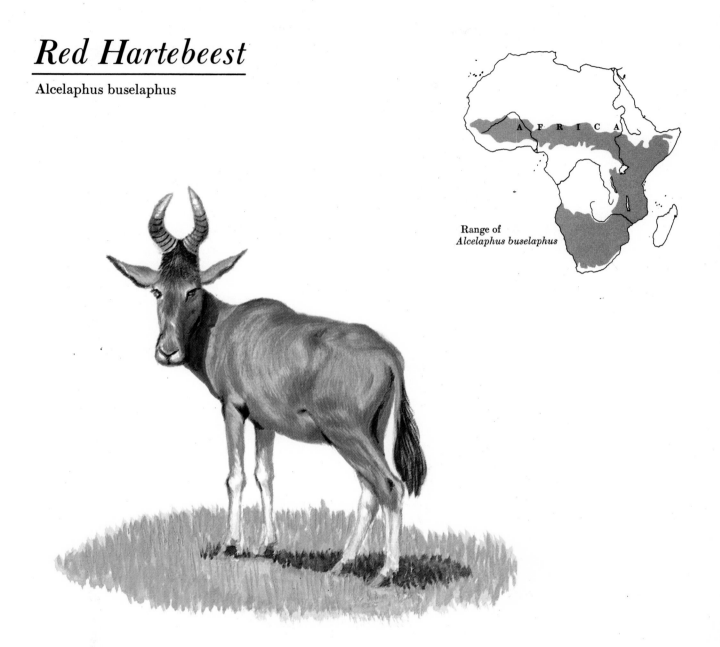

Range of
Alcelaphus buselaphus

A GREGARIOUS PLAINS-DWELLER. A mixed herd of hartebeests and wildebeests, zebras and waterbucks thundering over the grasslands of Africa offers a unique picture of color and motion. But the hartebeests are not always in strange company; just as often they form their own herds of six to 20 individuals, and to see them on the move is equally spectacular. Warned by a sentry on a hilltop that danger threatens, the big antelopes dash away in single file; since their rumps slope backwards from their shoulder humps their gait is awkward and clumsy but they have been clocked to attain a speed of 40 miles per hour. The range of the two species — the red and Lichtenstein's hartebeests — runs southward from a line between Senegal in West Africa and Somaliland in the east. Another species, extinct since the early 20th century, roamed all of Africa in the days of antiquity; the Romans called it "a horned horse." The head and body of the hartebeest may grow to a length of 6½ feet with a shoulder height of 5 feet and a weight of 400 pounds. The color of the fine-textured coat is brownish-grayish-reddish; the red species has white markings on shoulders and other parts of the body. Both males and females carry ringed horns which grow from a single base. The horns are not used as weapons since the hartebeests hardly ever fight, even when injured or cornered. Although the horns are picturesquely lyre-shaped they are not considered a desirable trophy by big game hunters. On the open plains or among shrubs the animals graze in the morning and late afternoon. The one young has a life expectancy of up to 20 years.

Range of
Connochaetes taurinus

WILDEBEEST OR WILD BEAST. This is the gnu's alternate name, but the Dutch colonists who coined this savage-sounding word were slyly misled. The animals look indeed ferocious, with their shaggy manes and straggly beards, bristly hairs in their horse-like faces and strong recurved horns on both bulls and cows. When a human being approaches them they give a threatening performance, kicking and pawing the dust, prancing on their four legs, thrashing their tails and stabbing the earth with their horns. However, there is no need to be afraid. At a closer approach they rush off and at a safe distance turn around, face their adversary again and repeat the show; they never go beyond bluffing. The gnu will attain a head-and-body length of 6½ feet, with a shoulder height of 4 feet and a weight of up to 600 pounds; its silvery-gray skin shows brown bands on shoulders, neck, and the front part of the body while face, beard and tail are black. Gnus live on the grasslands that stretch from Kenya southward, in herds of five to 100 individuals. Females have four nipples but only a single young.

White-bearded Gnu

Connochaetes taurinus

Klipspringer

Oreotragus oreotragus

Range of
Oreotragus oreotragus

THE CLIFF-SPRINGING ANTELOPE. A klipspringer standing still and unconcerned high up against the African sky, on a stony projection the size of a dollar coin; its four round hoofs touching each other, its horns pointing straight up between the alert ears, and its thick coat glowing in yellow-brown-orange — that is a delightful sight. In the mountain regions of tropical Africa it moves, in groups of two to eight, over the rocky wastes at an incredible speed, without apparent footholds, like the mountain goats of the Rockies or the chamois of the Alps. In harmony with its dry habitat it does not have to drink regularly, and the dense coat with its moss-like hair is wrapped around it like a mat which protects against bruises and injuries. So elastic is the hair that in former days riding saddles were stuffed with it. The klipspringer's head and body may reach a length of a little over 3 feet, with a shoulder height of 2 feet and a weight of 35½ pounds. Its shrill whistle may express either inquisitiveness or alarm.

Pygmy Antelope

Neotragus batesi

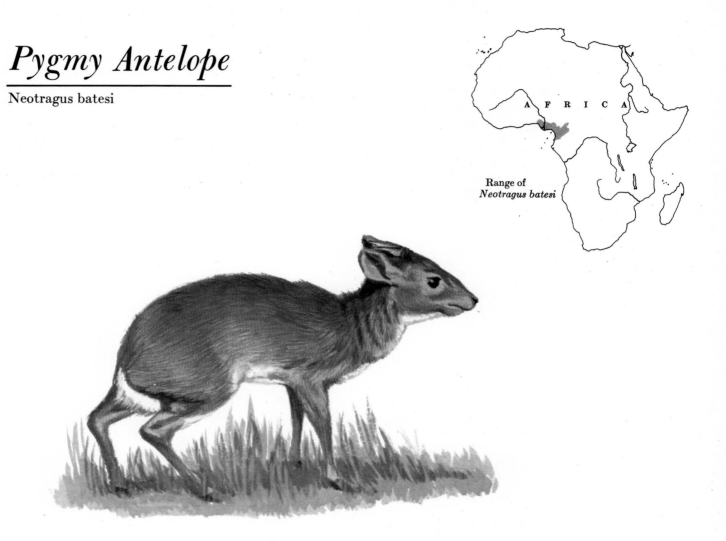

A F R I C A

Range of
Neotragus batesi

THE SMALLEST HOOFED ANIMAL. The name pygmy or dwarf antelope seems to fit this African mammal better than the high-sounding "royal antelope." It is true that single individuals of the Asiatic mouse deer may even be tinier, but as a genus the *Neotragus* antelopes are the smallest members of the family *Bovidae*. The two species of the genus are neighbors; the one living in Sierra Leone and Liberia east to Nigeria (*pygmaeus*) stands 9½ to 12 inches high at the shoulders. Its smooth horns, carried only by males, are black and approximately one inch long; head and body grow to a length of 19½ inches. The second species (*batesi*) inhabits the forests east of the Niger River and the jungles of the Cameroon. Its shoulder height is about 14 inches; the horns of the males are brown and grow to a length of two inches. Both species are cinnamon-colored above and white below. They live singly or in pairs and mate at any time of the year. The natives catch them in traps set near patches of peanut plants. According to Liberian folklore they are smart,

quick and resourceful little animals; there they play the role performed by "Br'er Rabbit" in the American South. Another lilliputian antelope which has created folklore tales and superstitions is the dik-dik (genus *Madoqua*). This yellowish-grayish-brownish dweller of brush areas is 21 to 26 inches long, with a shoulder height of 16 inches. When excited, it utters a call sounding like "dik-dik" while it trots off in a sequence of erratic jumps, zigzag style. The males have ringed horns. The genus inhabits two disconnected ranges, one in eastern Africa, the other in South-West Africa and Angola. Neither the Bushmen nor the Baketes of the Congo kill them, in the belief that loss of teeth and other evils will follow the eating of dik-dik meat. However, the pygmies of the Ituri Forest in the northeastern part of the Congo trap considerable numbers of them, hang them on sticks and sell them by the road. Big game hunters complain that the dik-diks flush and alert the large animals. Pictured here is the eastern royal antelope.

INDIA'S FAVORITE GAME. Traditionally India's sportsmen have been fond of chasing the blackbuck, for its meat is tasty, its horns are a marvelous trophy, and the hunt is difficult. Blackbucks are wary and alert, especially the females. At the first sign of danger one member of the herd gives the warning signal by bouncing high into the air; others follow, and a few moments later the whole herd is in a state of commotion. When they run off they are so fleet that only one pursuer is able to catch them — the cheetah. For centuries cheetahs have been trained in India to capture and hold the blackbuck until the master arrives. The range of these antelopes extends from western Pakistan through the Punjab to Bengal in the east, and south to Cape Comorin, the southern tip of the Indian peninsula. They inhabit the open plains, not mountain areas or forests. The head-and-body length of an adult male is approximately 4 feet, with a weight of 82 pounds. The underparts of both bucks and does are white but while the females have a yellowish coloration on head and back, the upper parts and the outside legs of the males are deep brown; in the distance the color seems black which suggests the animal's name. Both have white patches around their eyes. The horns of the bucks (the does are hornless) are most handsome. Decorated with rings at the base, they twist upward in four or five spirals, to a length of 27 inches. Herds consist of 15 to 50 members, usually led by a single buck. During the mating season in February and March the males courageously fight all rivals and intruders including human beings. Blackbucks feed by day on the short grasses of the plains and on various cereals.

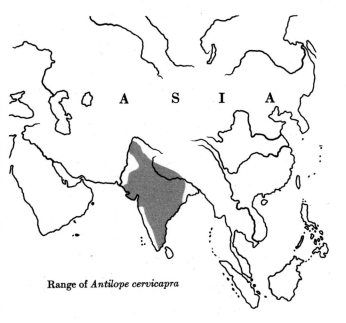

Range of *Antilope cervicapra*

Blackbuck

Antilope cervicapra

THE HIGH JUMP CHAMPION. To watch a troop of twenty impalas leap high over a cluster of bushes, all at the same time, is an unforgettable experience, a spectacle of effortless grace, a flight rather than a jump. Sometimes these light-footed animals perform a sequence of several leaps while running over the plains; one continuity which was measured consisted of three bounds of 25, 15 and 30 feet. Often they jump for the joy of it, over each other, or just up into the air if no hurdle challenges them. The range of the impalas stretches southward from Kenya and Uganda to South Africa; the open forest and the acacia-savannas are their habitat. There they spend their lives, active both during the day and at night, now grazing or browsing, now resting and sleeping. Once every day they visit a water hole to drink. When danger threatens from lions or other predators, they rather seek safety in hiding in the underbrush than in flight. The head-and-body length of an adult male is approximately 5 feet with a weight of about 165 pounds. The sleek and shiny hair is reddish above, white below. A black band runs vertically over each side of the hindquarters. The males only carry handsome, lyre-shaped horns with front ridges, as long as two and a half feet. During the dry season huge herds of hundreds of impalas gather but later in the year separate into harem-groups consisting of one strong buck and 15 to 25 females. During mating time in April and May the males often fight ferociously with each other. Five and one-half to six months later one or two young are born.

Impala

Aepyceros melampus

A F R I C A

Range of
Aepyceros melampus

Gerenuk

Litocranius walleri

A TREE-FEEDING GAZELLE. The oldest pictures of a gerenuk are found in ancient Egyptian tombs. Apparently the unusual habits of this animal have arrested human attention since time immemorial. Its feeding stance is indeed queer. It stands on its long hind legs, its forelegs pressed against the tree; its body points straight up, and its long tongue plucks leaves from the acacia branches. When sensing danger it hides behind trees and bushes in a motionless pose; then the long giraffe-like neck appears above the cover like a periscope to survey the scene. When it runs, head, neck, body and tail form a horizontal streamline. The Somalis consider the gerenuks relatives of the camel; therefore they do not kill and eat them for fear that harm to the gerenuks will mean death to their camels. The range of this gazelle extends through eastern Africa, from Somaliland to Kenya. The head-and-body length of an adult male is approximately 5 feet, with a weight of up to 110 pounds. The upper parts of its body are reddish, the front of the neck and the lower parts are white; a broad brown "blanket" covers the back and the upper sides. Only the male has horns; they curve backwards and end with a forward hook.

Range of
Litocranius walleri

Springbuck

Antidorcas marsupialis

Range of
Antidorcas marsupialis

TRAGIC MIGRANT. Before South Africa was densely settled, spectacular migrations of springbucks took place whenever a drought depleted the food supply. Herds estimated at a million individuals moved across the country; it would take several days for such a multitude to pass a given landmark. Ruined crops lay in their wake, and the government distributed rifles to destroy the migrants by the tens of thousands. Myriads of others were shot by poachers, their meat sold as biltong, i.e., dried and cured. In consequence of this tragic destruction the springbuck has become very rare, and while its original range comprised the treeless plains of the Kalahari desert, Angola and South Africa, it is now confined to a few South African parks. An adult specimen has a head-and-body length of approximately 4½ feet, with a weight of about 80 pounds. Between the cinnamon-colored upper and the white lower parts, a reddish-brown horizontal band extends along each side. Black ringed horns adorn both males and females. The animal's name has been derived from a curious habit: When surprised or at a game the springbuck suddenly leaps into the air for 10 or 11 feet, curving its body and holding its legs close together. It also bounds across roads and wagon trails since it distrusts the marks of man. It feeds mainly on grass and karoo shrubs, and does not seem to need water.

LIFE ABOVE THE TIMBERLINE. Moving slowly over the sky-high wastelands of the Rockies and the coastal ranges of Canada and Alaska, the Rocky Mountain goat is well-equipped for its cold environment. Its sturdy body with a length of approximately 5 feet may weigh up to 310 pounds, and the white or yellowish outer fur is strengthened by a thick and woolly underfur. Stiff hairs form a ridge on the neck, and the hoofs have sharp, strong rims which enclose a soft pad, an effective arrangement for moving on stony and icy ground. Both males and females have black, conical horns, approximately one foot long. Although not graceful animals, these goat-antelopes are sure-footed climbers and remarkable jumpers. In mountain areas above the timberline they feed on grasses, lichens, and the leaves of trees and shrubs. To reach salt licks they will travel for miles. Deep snow is their greatest danger, and snowslides kill a good number of them. During the season of heaviest snowfall they descend to lower valleys and sometimes find shelter in caves. Two young are born between April and June; they are sturdy and able to jump when only 30 minutes old; quite a few are caught by cougars, bears, wolves and eagles. They are also legal game animals in various western regions. In 1924 a herd of Rocky Mountain goats was transplanted to the Black Hills of South Dakota where they are thriving.

Range of
Oreamnos americanus

Rocky Mountain Goat

Oreamnos americanus

Chamois

Rupicapra rupicapra

Range of *Rupicapra rupicapra*

GRACEFUL SYMBOL OF THE ALPS. No mountain animal has been described in European folklore and literature with more admiration than the chamois. It is nimble, sure-footed and daring, leaping over precipitous stone walls to the most inaccessible crags when alarmed. The sentinel of the herd has a special danger signal; it whistles sharply while stamping its feet. The chamois is hunted not only for its excellent meat but also for its hide, the source of the superbly supple "shammy leather." The long winter hair is worked into the brushes which decorate Tyrolean hats. While best known in the Alps, the chamois occurs also on all other high mountain ranges of Europe and Asia Minor. The head-and-body length of a male may reach 4 feet, with a weight of up to 310 pounds. The summer coat is short and tawny, the winter hair woolly, up to seven and one-half inches long, and blackish-brown. These mountaineers live in herds of up to 30 females and young, joined by the males only at mating time. One young is the rule; in case of the mother's death the other females raise the orphan, a custom which has contributed to the strong survival of the species.

CATTLE OF THE ARCTIC NORTH. On the treeless tundras and bleak snowfields of northern Canada and Greenland the clumsy-looking but agile musk ox lives in herds that may include as many as 100 members. Strong and courageous, it never tries to escape when danger threatens; instead, the adults form a circle around the calves, their bulky heads lowered toward the outside and their sharp horns threatening. This formidable defense array discourages packs of wolves, but these oxen have not learned that in their defensive position they also offer fixed targets for so-called sportsmen who may easily slaughter the whole herd. Up to 7½ feet long, with a maximum weight of 900 pounds, the musk ox is perfectly equipped for the Arctic life; its dark-brown outer hairs, which shed snow and rain, almost touch the ground. Below, a thick, soft, light-brown inner coat is impenetrable to moisture and cold. The front and the lower parts are black, the short legs are light. The horns, growing from the center of the skull, turn sharply downward. Scratching through the snow, these large beasts manage to gather sufficient vegetable matter for survival in a harsh environment.

Range of
Ovibos moschatus

Musk Ox

Ovibos moschatus

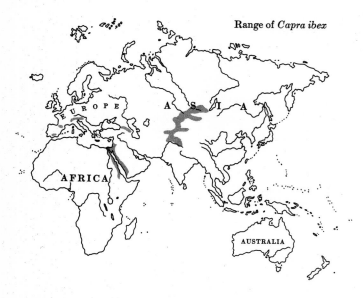

Range of *Capra ibex*

WILD GOATS OF THE OLD WORLD. The five species of wild goats which include the ibexes have an enormous range. South of the Mediterranean it comprises Egypt and Arabia, Ethiopia and the Sudan; north of that sea it reaches from Spain eastward to India and north to Siberia. All wild goats are handsome, powerful animals with massive, heavily ridged horns; one of them, the Alpine ibex, has actually become an object of awe and mystery. The German version of its name is "Steinbock," which in turn is applied to the tenth sign of the zodiac, Capricorn. In Germany, Austria and Switzerland a whole body of astrological folklore has been built around this animal. Not only have its horns and its blood found their way into pharmacies as medicines and potions but also the balls of indigestible hair which occasionally are vomited by the Steinbock were preserved and sometimes gilded. Another folk story asserts that the Steinbock carries a cross in its heart, and it does. At least several of its flat heart cartilages happen to grow in the form of a cross. In spite of its aura the Alpine ibex has been badly overhunted; in its natural state it survives only in Italy's Gran Paradiso National Park; from here the Austrian and Swiss preserves have been restocked.

Ibex

Capra ibex

Markhor

Capra (or Orthaegoceros) falconeri

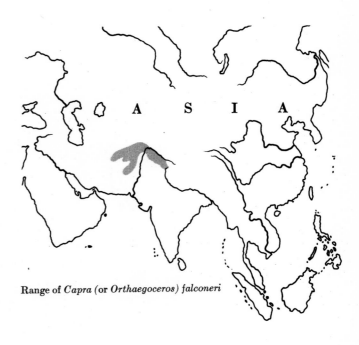

Range of *Capra (or Orthaegoceros) falconeri*

A GRAND TROPHY. One of Asia's wild goats, the markhor, is immediately recognized by its magnificent horns; they stand in an upright V and have been described as a "flattish spiral." The markhor's long fur clothes neck and shoulders and hangs down on its chest; the coloration is gray and brown, with whitish underparts in some races. Its range comprises western Pakistan, Afghanistan, Kashmir, and the southern part of Soviet Central Asia; there the markhor lives in rough and broken mountain territory in small herds of 15 to 20 individuals, usually led by an old and experienced female. In seasonal migrations the herds leave the snow of the winter and descend to the valleys; in spring they return to the meadows just below the snow line. Being nocturnal, they become active in the afternoon and graze on grasses or browse on leaves all night. Like the adult males of all species of wild goats the markhors attain a head-and-body length of 5 feet, with a weight of up to 265 pounds; the females grow to only half that size and weight. An age of 10 to 18 years has been reported as their life-span. The domesticated goat is a descendant of the wild goats which live in the Caucasus, Iran, Asia Minor and on the Greek islands; it is estimated that the domestication took place eight or nine thousand years ago.

AFRICA'S ONLY WILD SHEEP. Around the Sahara, from the Atlantic shore to the Red Sea and south to the Sudan the Barbary sheep or aoudad lives in barren, rocky and waterless terrain. It is a sure-footed climber using the smallest ridges as footholds while searching for stunted bushes and other plant growth. Watercourses are practically absent in its territory, so it is content with the moisture in leaves and the dew of the cold desert nights. Since there are no trees or thickets in which to hide in case of danger, these sheep remain completely motionless, melting into the rocky landscape with their tawny fur. A male adult will grow to a length of 6 feet and a weight of 250 pounds; a feature which distinguishes it from all other wild sheep is a plumelike fringe of long hair which hangs down from throat, chest and forelegs. The horns, sweeping outward, backward and inward, are up to 33 inches long and a handsome trophy; those of the females are smaller. A combat between two rams is spectacular; from starting positions 40 or 50 feet apart the fighters first walk and then run against each other, their heads lowered. With a crash of their horns they collide; but in a chivalrous gesture no ram will attack an adversary who is unsuspecting. In desert life the sheep's meat and hide, hair and sinews are important to the natives and the animals are hunted extensively. In an experiment of acclimatization Barbary sheep have been introduced to the southwestern United States.

Range of
Ammotragus lervia

Barbary Sheep

Ammotragus lervia

Bighorn Sheep

Ovis canadensis

ON PRECIPICES AND CRAGS ABOVE THE CLOUDS. In the mountainous sections of western America, from British Columbia and Saskatchewan south to New Mexico and east to the Black Hills of South Dakota the bighorn sheep prefer to stay on the most precipitous and dangerous rocky wastes and snowfields. In the Rockies they never descend to the tree line and rarely visit the high alpine meadows. For shelter they select ledges which offer a broad panoramic view of the surrounding countryside. The females give birth to their one to three young in the privacy of the roughest and most inaccessible crags. The head-and-body length of an adult male is approximately 6 feet, with a weight of up to 440 pounds. The thick coat varies in color from creamy-white to yellowish-gray to dull brown. The horns of the male are heavy and spiral, those of the female short and slightly bent. The males stay by themselves in small herds and the females graze with their young. In the fall harems are formed, and in the mating combat of the rams some males are killed. Grasses, leaves and other plant materials are part of their diet; during the winter they have to subsist on the meager alpine vegetation where blizzards have blown away the snow.

Range of
Ovis canadensis

ISLAND-DWELLER. The handsome mouflon with its reddish coat, white belly and deeply curved horns which almost touch its shoulders is a characteristic feature of the islands of Corsica and Sardinia. There it lives in small flocks in rugged mountain areas, hill forests and stony thickets. The home territory to which it is indigenous may be small, but the mouflon's significance lies in the fact that it has been widely introduced to continental Europe, particularly to central European mountain ranges. The Soviet Union has acclimatized mouflons, and the Krimskiy National Park on the Crimean Peninsula in the Black Sea preserves several herds. The males live in flocks by themselves; the females and young form their own groups. When confronted with danger they utter a snorting noise but then bound away over crags and boulders with graceful ease. The mouflon is a sheep and as such is quite closely related to the goats. There are, however, several conspicuous distinctions: the forehead of the goat is convex, that of the sheep is concave; goats have beards but neither sheep, ewes nor rams have them; the male goat exudes a strong odor while the male sheep is odorless. The mouflon is distinguished from all other sheep by growing a dense undercoat during the winter; however, it is not visible under the coarse outer coat. None of the wild sheep have the wool-producing capacity of the domestic sheep, and if runaway sheep revert to the wilderness they are said to lose their woolly fur and grow a coat of rough hair.

Range of *Ovis musimon*

Mouflon

Ovis musimon

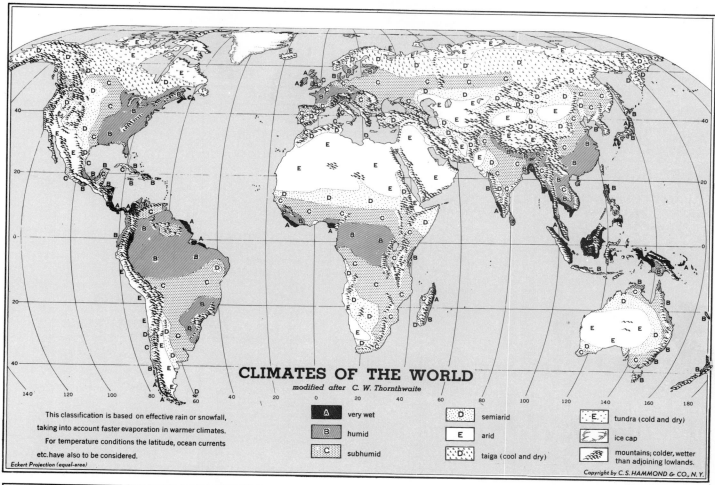

CLIMATES OF THE WORLD
modified after C. W. Thornthwaite

This classification is based on effective rain or snowfall,
taking into account faster evaporation in warmer climates.
For temperature conditions the latitude, ocean currents
etc. have also to be considered.

Eckert Projection (equal-area)

A	very wet
B	humid
C	subhumid
D	semiarid
E	arid
D	taiga (cool and dry)
E	tundra (cold and dry)
	ice cap
	mountains; colder, wetter than adjoining lowlands.

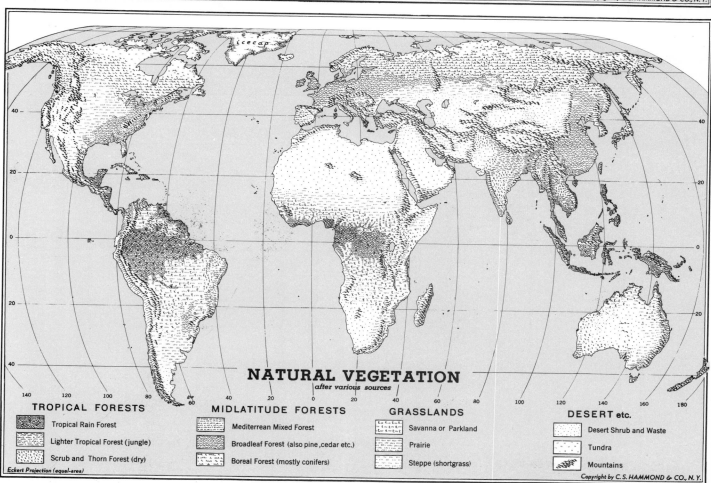

NATURAL VEGETATION
after various sources

TROPICAL FORESTS
- Tropical Rain Forest
- Lighter Tropical Forest (jungle)
- Scrub and Thorn Forest (dry)

MIDLATITUDE FORESTS
- Mediterrean Mixed Forest
- Broadleaf Forest (also pine, cedar etc.)
- Boreal Forest (mostly conifers)

GRASSLANDS
- Savanna or Parkland
- Prairie
- Steppe (shortgrass)

DESERT etc.
- Desert Shrub and Waste
- Tundra
- Mountains

Eckert Projection (equal-area)

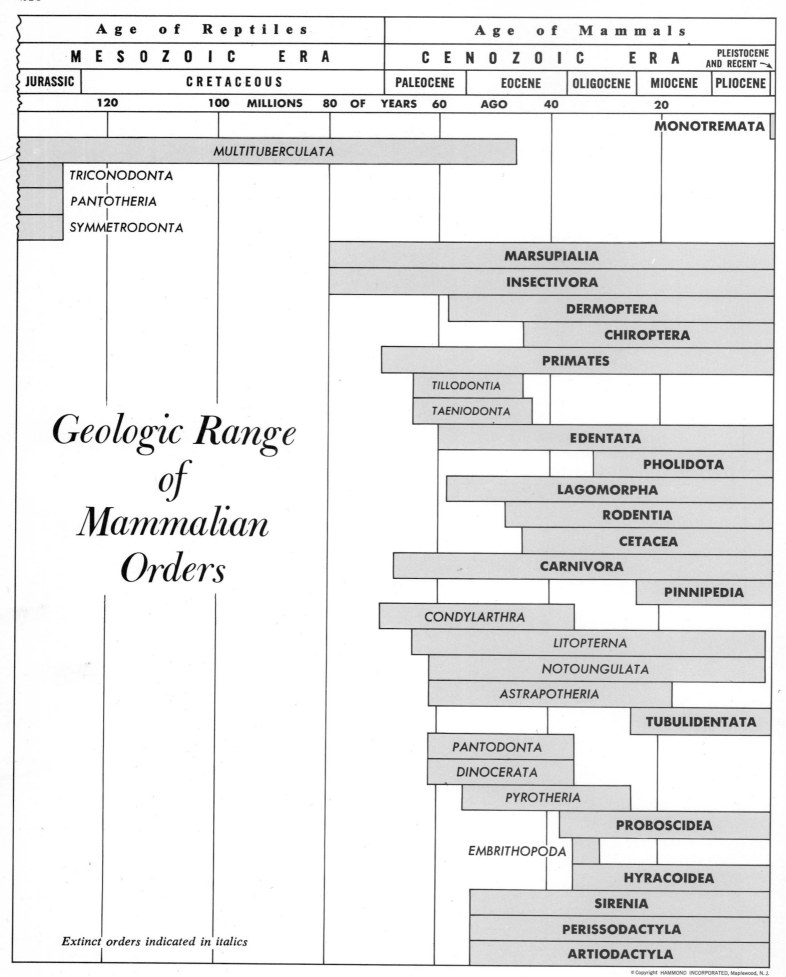

210

Age of Reptiles | Age of Mammals

MESOZOIC ERA | CENOZOIC ERA | PLEISTOCENE AND RECENT →

JURASSIC | CRETACEOUS | PALEOCENE | EOCENE | OLIGOCENE | MIOCENE | PLIOCENE

120   100 MILLIONS 80 OF YEARS 60 AGO 40   20

MONOTREMATA

MULTITUBERCULATA

TRICONODONTA

PANTOTHERIA

SYMMETRODONTA

MARSUPIALIA

INSECTIVORA

DERMOPTERA

CHIROPTERA

PRIMATES

TILLODONTIA

TAENIODONTA

Geologic Range of Mammalian Orders

EDENTATA

PHOLIDOTA

LAGOMORPHA

RODENTIA

CETACEA

CARNIVORA

PINNIPEDIA

CONDYLARTHRA

LITOPTERNA

NOTOUNGULATA

ASTRAPOTHERIA

TUBULIDENTATA

PANTODONTA

DINOCERATA

PYROTHERIA

PROBOSCIDEA

EMBRITHOPODA

HYRACOIDEA

SIRENIA

PERISSODACTYLA

Extinct orders indicated in italics

ARTIODACTYLA

Classification of Mammals

The *class* of vertebrate animals called Mammalia consists of three *subclasses,* Prototheria, Allotheria and Theria. Prototheria is composed of but one *order,* Monotremata, with but two *families,* and Allotheria has only two extinct orders. The order Triconodonta is of uncertain position between Allotheria and Theria, so is listed under both subclasses. All of the remaining orders of extinct and living mammals are contained in subclass Theria. This classification includes all generally accepted living and extinct (printed in *italic* type) orders, and all living families. Under the families are listed just those *species* illustrated in this book, with the appropriate text pages. References to additional *genera* and species mentioned in the text may be found in the index, which contains a list of all technical and popular names included in the book.

Changes in all ranks of classification occur frequently, and even new orders are occasionally proposed. Leading authorities often disagree in their acceptance of certain *taxonomic* (name classification) forms, and in their particular position within a family or order. The total number of genera and species noted in this list, therefore, refers to only living members of the class. The widest range of numbers according to the latest and most authoritative sourcebooks dealing with mammals and their classification is shown, and those noted as "recent" by some authors are not included, as they are actually extinct today.

The orders and families follow generally accepted evolutionary positions, from the oldest to those believed to be of most recent development. The illustrated species noted under the family headings, however, are arranged alphabetically by genera within each family, enabling the reader to find the names more easily.

class **MAMMALIA**

subclass **PROTOTHERIA**

order **MONOTREMATA:** egg-laying mammals (2 families, 3 genera, 6 species)

    families: TACHYGLOSSIDAE: echidnas (2 genera, 5 species)
          Tachyglossus aculeatus — echidna or spiny anteater (page 18)

        ORNITHORHYNCHIDAE: platypus (1 genus, 1 species)
          Ornithorhynchus anatinus — duck-billed platypus (page 19)

subclass **ALLOTHERIA**

order **MULTITUBERCULATA**

order **TRICONODONTA (?)**

subclass **THERIA**

order **TRICONODONTA (?)**

order **PANTOTHERIA**

order **SYMMETRODONTA**

order **MARSUPIALIA:** pouched mammals or marsupials (8-9 families, 79-81 genera, 223-248 species)

    families: DIDELPHIDAE: American opossums (12 genera, 55-66 species)
          Didelphis marsupialis — common American or Virginia opossum (page 20)

        DASYURIDAE: flesh-eating marsupials (19-20 genera, 45-50 species)
          (including the numbat (1 genus, 1 species) , sometimes separated
          as family MYRMECOBIIDAE)
          Dasyurus quoll — Australian "native cat" or eastern dasyure (page 21)
          Sarcophilus harrisii — Tasmanian devil (page 22)
          Thylacinus cynocephalus — Tasmanian "wolf" (page 23)

        NOTORYCTIDAE: marsupial "moles" (1 genus, 1-2 species)

        PERAMELIDAE: insect-eating marsupials or bandicoots (8 genera, 19-22 species)
          Perameles fasciata — eastern barred bandicoot (page 24)

        CAENOLESTIDAE: rat opossums (3 genera, 7 species)

        PHALANGERIDAE: phalangers and relatives (16-19 genera, 42-52 species)
          Petaurus breviceps — lesser gliding possum or squirrel-like
           flying phalanger (page 26)
          Phalanger maculatus — spotted cuscus (page 25)
          Phascolarctos cinereus — koala or "teddy bear" (page 27)

        PHASCOLOMIDAE (PHASCOLOMYIDAE or VOMBATIDAE):
          wombats (2 genera, 2 species)
          Phascolomis ursinus — common wombat (page 28)

        MACROPODIDAE: kangaroos and wallabies (17-19 genera, 47-55 species)
          Dendrolagus bennettianus — dusky or Bennet's tree kangaroo (page 31)
          Macropus giganteus — great gray kangaroo (page 30)
          Wallabia rufogrisea — red-necked wallaby (page 29)

order **INSECTIVORA:** insect-eating mammals or insectivores (7-9 families, 62-72 genera, 292-391 species)
          (excluding family TUPAIIDAE, sometimes included here
          (see PRIMATES) , and excluding family *NESOPHONTIDAE* (1 genus, 6 species) ,
          the West Indian shrews, "possibly still living" according to a few sources)

milies: SOLENODONTIDAE: solenodons (1-2 genera, 2 species)

TENRECIDAE: tenrecs (10-11 genera, 20-30 species)

POTAMOGALIDAE: African water or otter shrews (2 genera, 3 species)
(sometimes included with TENRECIDAE)

CHRYSOCHLORIDAE: golden moles (5 genera, 11-20 species)

ERINACEIDAE: hedgehogs (8-10 genera, 14-20 species)

MACROSCELIDIDAE: elephant shrews (4-5 genera, 18-28 species)

SORICIDAE: shrews (20-24 genera, 200-291 species)
Sorex cinereus — long-tailed shrew (page 32)

TALPIDAE: moles (12-15 genera, 19-22 species)
Condylura cristata — star-nosed mole (page 34)
Talpa europaea — common Eurasian mole (page 33)

PTERA: "flying" lemurs or colugos (1 family, 1 genus, 2 species)

amily: CYNOCEPHALIDAE: "flying" lemurs or colugos (1 genus, 2 species)
Cynocephalus variegatus — "flying" lemur or East Indian colugo (page 36)

PTERA: flying mammals or bats (16-17 families, 173-182 genera, 797-980 species)
(composed of two suborders, the Megachiroptera, comprising only the
first family and the Microchiroptera, containing all of the other families
in the order)

milies: PTEROPODIDAE (or PTEROPIDAE): Old World fruit bats (38-39 genera, 130-154 species)
Pteropus vampyrus — flying "fox" or fruit bat (page 37)

RHINOPOMATIDAE: mouse-tailed bats (1 genus, 3-4 species)

EMBALLONURIDAE: sac-winged and ghost bats (12-13 genera, 40-52 species)

NOCTILIONIDAE: bulldog bats (1 genus, 2 species)

NYCTERIDAE: slit-faced or hispid bats (1 genus, 10-20 species)

MEGADERMATIDAE (or MEGADERMIDAE): false vampire and yellow-winged bats
(3-4 genera, 5 species)

RHINOLOPHIDAE: horseshoe bats (2 genera, 51-75 species)

HIPPOSIDERIDAE: Old World leaf-nosed bats (9 genera, 40-66 species)
(sometimes included with RHINOLOPHIDAE)

PHYLLOSTOMIDAE (or PHYLLOSTOMATIDAE): New World leaf-nosed
bats (50-53 genera, 129-143 species)

DESMODONTIDAE: vampire bats (3 genera, 3 species)
Desmodus rotundus — common vampire bat (page 38)

NATALIDAE: funnel-eared bats (1 genus, 4-11 species)

FURIPTERIDAE: smoky bats (2 genera, 2 species)

THYROPTERIDAE: disk-winged bats (1 genus, 2 species)

MYZOPODIDAE: sucker-footed bat (1 genus, 1 species)

VESPERTILIONIDAE: common bats (35-39 genera, 275-324 species)

MYSTACINIDAE: New Zealand short-tailed bat (1 genus, 1 species)

MOLOSSIDAE: free-tailed or mastiff bats (10-12 genera, 80-119 species)

order **PRIMATES:** primates, or monkeys, apes and man and relatives (10-12 families, 52-80 genera, 180-244 species)

families: TUPAIIDAE: tree shrews (5-6 genera, 15-31 species)
(sometimes included with order INSECTIVORA)

LEMURIDAE: lemurs (5-6 genera, 15-16 species)

INDRIDAE: woolly lemurs (3 genera, 4 species)

DAUBENTONIIDAE: aye-aye (1 genus, 1 species)

LORISIDAE: lorises and relatives (6 genera, 11-12 species)
(including the galagos (3 genera, 6 species), sometimes separated
as family GALAGIDAE)
Nycticebus coucang — slow loris (page 40)

TARSIIDAE: tarsiers (1 genus, 3 species)
Tarsius syrichta — Philippine tarsier (page 41)

CEBIDAE: New World monkeys (11-12 genera, 29-43 species)
Alouatta seniculus — red howler (page 42)
Ateles geoffroyi — red spider monkey or mico (page 44)
Cebus capucinus — white-faced capuchin or sapajou (page 43)
Lagothrix lagotricha — common woolly monkey (page 45)

CALLITHRICIDAE: marmosets and tamarins (4 genera, 33-35 species)
Leontideus rosalia — golden or lion-headed marmoset (page 46)
Saguinus oedipus — cotton-head marmoset or pinché (page 47)

CERCOPITHECIDAE: Old World monkeys (11-29 genera, 60-86 species)
Cercocebus torquatus — red-crowned mangabey (page 51)
Cercopithecus aethiops — guenon (page 55)
Chaeropithecus ursinus — Chacma baboon (page 52)
Colobus polykomos — black and white colobus monkey or guereza (page 58)
Comopithecus hamadryas — hamadryas or sacred baboon (page 53)
Macaca mulatta — rhesus monkey or macaque (page 48)
Macaca nemestrina — pig-tailed macaque (page 50)
Macaca sylvanus — Barbary ape (page 49)
Mandrillus sphinx — mandrill (page 54)
Nasalis larvatus — proboscis monkey (page 57)
Presbytis entellus — common Indian langur (page 56)

PONGIDAE: anthropoid apes (4-5 genera, 8-10 species)
Gorilla gorilla — gorilla (page 63)
Hylobates hoolock — hoolock gibbon (page 59)
Hylobates lar — white-handed gibbon or lar (page 60)
Pan troglodytes — chimpanzee (page 62)
Pongo pygmaeus — orangutan (page 61)

HOMINIDAE: man (1 genus, 1 species)

order *TILLODONTIA*

order *TAENIODONTA*

order **EDENTATA:** anteaters, tree sloths and armadillos or edentates (3 families, 14 genera, 30-32 species)

families: MYRMECOPHAGIDAE: anteaters (3 genera, 3-4 species)
Myrmecophaga tridactyla — giant anteater (page 65)

BRADYPODIDAE: tree sloths (2 genera, 6-7 species)
Choloepus hoffmanni — two-toed or Hoffmann's sloth (page 66)

DASYPODIDAE: armadillos (9 genera, 20-21 species)
Priodontes giganteus — giant armadillo (page 67)
Tolypeutes matacus — La Plata three-banded armadillo (page 68)

order **PHOLIDOTA:** scaled mammals or pangolins (1 family, 1 genus, 7-8 species)

    family: MANIDAE: pangolins (1 genus, 7-8 species)
        Manis gigantea — giant pangolin (page 69)

order **LAGOMORPHA:** leaping mammals or pikas, rabbits and hares (2 families, 9-10 genera, 63-66 species)

    families: OCHOTONIDAE: pikas or conies (1 genus, 14 species)
        Ochotona princeps — American pika or little chief hare (page 71)

        LEPORIDAE: rabbits and hares (8-9 genera, 49-52 species)
        Lepus townsendi — white-tailed jack rabbit (page 72)
        Oryctolagus cuniculus — Old World rabbit (page 73)

order **RODENTIA:** gnawing mammals or rodents (32-33 families, 346-368 genera, 1,685-1,844 species)

    families: APLODONTIIDAE (or APLODONTIDAE): mountain beaver or sewellel (1 genus, 1 species)

        SCIURIDAE: squirrels (44-51 genera, 245-261 species)
        Cynomys ludovicianus — plains prairie "dog" (page 75)
        Sciurus carolinensis — eastern gray squirrel (page 74)
        Tamias striatus — eastern American chipmunk (page 76)

        GEOMYIDAE: pocket gophers (8-9 genera, 30-40 species)

        HETEROMYIDAE: pocket mice and kangaroo rats (5 genera, 70-75 species)

        CASTORIDAE: beavers (1 genus, 1-2 species)
        Castor canadensis — American beaver (page 77)

        ANOMALURIDAE: scaly-tailed squirrels (4 genera, 9-12 species)

        PEDETIDAE: springhaas or springhares (1 genus, 1-2 species)

        CRICETIDAE: New World mice and rats, voles, and relatives (97-101 genera, 567-602 species)
        Dicrostonyx groenlandicus — Greenland lemming (page 78)
        Mesocricetus auratus — golden hamster (page 79)
        Ondatra zibethicus — common muskrat (page 80)

        SPALACIDAE: mole rats (1 genus, 3 species)

        RHIZOMYIDAE: bamboo rats (3 genera, 18 species)

        MURIDAE: Old World mice, rats and relatives (98-106 genera, 457-493 species)
        Mus musculus — house mouse (page 82)
        Rattus norvegicus — brown or Norway rat (page 81)

        GLIRIDAE: dormice (7 genera, 10-28 species)

        PLATACANTHOMYIDAE: spiny dormice (2 genera, 2 species)

        SELEVINIIDAE: desert dormouse or dzhalman (1 genus, 1 species)

        ZAPODIDAE: jumping mice (4 genera, 11 species)

        DIPODIDAE: jerboas (10 genera, 25-27 species)

        HYSTRICIDAE: Old World or terrestrial porcupines (4 genera, 15-20 species)

        ERETHIZONTIDAE: New World or arboreal porcupines (4 genera, 8-23 species)
        Erethizon dorsatum — North American porcupine (page 83)

        CAVIIDAE: cavies or guinea pigs (3-6 genera, 12-23 species)
        Cavia porcellus — cavy or guinea pig (page 84)

        HYDROCHOERIDAE: capybaras (1 genus, 1-2 species)

        DINOMYIDAE: false paca or pacarana (1 genus, 1 species)

        DASYPROCTIDAE: agoutis and pacas (3-4 genera, 11-30 species)

CHINCHILLIDAE: chinchillas and viscachas (3 genera, 6-7 species)
Chinchilla laniger — chinchilla (page 85)

CAPROMYIDAE: hutias and coypu (4 genera, 8-12 species)
(including the coypu or nutria (1 genus, 1 species), sometimes separated as family MYOCASTORIDAE)

OCTODONTIDAE: hedge rats (5-6 genera, 8-9 species)

CTENOMYIDAE: tucotucos (1 genus, 26-27 species)

ABROCOMIDAE: chinchilla rats (1 genus, 2 species)

ECHIMYIDAE: spiny rats (14-15 genera, 43-69 species)

THRYONOMYIDAE: cane rats (1 genus, 2-6 species)

PETROMYIDAE: rock or dassie rat (1 genus, 1 species)

BATHYERGIDAE: mole rats (5 genera, 16-56 species)

CTENODACTYLIDAE: gundis (4 genera, 4-8 species)

order **CETACEA**: whales, dolphins and porpoises or cetaceans (8-10 families, 36-40 genera, 79-105 species)
(composed of two suborders, the Odontoceti, or toothed whales (first five families), and the Mysticeti, or whalebone whales (last three families)

families: PLATANISTIDAE: long-snouted river dolphins (3-4 genera, 3-4 species)
(including the Amazon and white flag dolphins (2 genera, 2 species), sometimes separated as family INIIDAE)

ZIPHIIDAE: beaked whales (5 genera, 14-18 species)

PHYSETERIDAE: sperm whales (2 genera, 2-3 species)
(including the pygmy sperm whales (1 genus, 1-2 species), sometimes separated as family KOGIIDAE)
Physeter catodon — sperm whale (page 87)

MONODONTIDAE: belugas and narwhal (2 genera, 2-3 species)

DELPHINIDAE: dolphins and porpoises (;8-20 genera, 48-64 species)
(including the rough-toothed, white and river dolphins (3 genera, 8-11 species), sometimes separated as family STENIDAE, and the common porpoises (3 genera, 3-7 species), sometimes separated as family PHOCOENIDAE)
Orcinus orca — killer whale (page 89)
Tursiops truncatus — common bottle-nosed dolphin (page 88)

ESCHRICHTIDAE (ESCHRICHTIIDAE, or RHACHIANECTIDAE):
gray whale (1 genus, 1 species)

BALAENOPTERIDAE: finback whales or rorquals (3 genera, 6 species)
Megaptera novaeangliae — humpback whale (page 90)
Sibbaldus musculus — blue or sulphur-bottom whale (page 91)

BALAENIDAE: right whales (2-3 genera, 3-6 species)

order **CARNIVORA**: terrestrial flesh-eating mammals or carnivores (7 families, 93-102 genera, 241-262 species)
(sometimes divided into two "tribes," the dogs and allies (the first four families), and the cats and allies (the last three families); the order is also sometimes called suborder Fissipedia when order Pinnipedia is included in CARNIVORA as a second suborder)

families: CANIDAE: dogs and relatives (14-15 genera, 35-41 species)
Alopex lagopus — Arctic fox (page 97)

Canis dingo — dingo (page 93)
Canis latrans — coyote (page 95)
Canis lupus — gray or timber wolf (page 94)
Canis mesomelas — black-backed jackal (page 96)
Cuon alpinus — dhole (page 102)
Fennecus zerda — fennec (page 99)
Lycaon pictus — Cape hunting dog (page 103)
Speothos venaticus — bush dog (page 101)
Urocyon cinereoargenteus — eastern gray fox (page 100)
Vulpes vulpes — common European red fox (page 98)

URSIDAE: bears (6-7 genera, 7-11 species)
Melursus ursinus — sloth bear (page 108)
Thalarctos maritimus — polar bear (page 107)
Ursus americanus — black bear (page 106)
Ursus arctos — grizzly or brown bear (page 105)
Ursus middendorffi — Kodiak or Alaskan brown bear (page 104)
(sometimes the last three named species are grouped into one
genus and two subgenera, then being called Ursus (Euarctos)
americanus, Ursus (Ursus) horribilis and Ursus (Ursus) middendorffi,
respectively; sometimes they are grouped into two genera and only two
species, then being called Euarctos americanus, Ursus arctos arctos and
Ursus arctos middendorffi, respectively)

PROCYONIDAE: raccoons and relatives (7-9 genera, 17-19 species)
Ailuropoda melanoleuca — giant panda (page 110)
Procyon lotor — common raccoon (page 109)

MUSTELIDAE: weasels, skunks and relatives (25-26 genera, 68-70 species)
Enhydra lutris — sea otter (page 121)
Lutra canadensis — Canadian otter (page 120)
Martes zibellina — Eurasian sable (page 114)
Mellivora capensis — honey badger or ratel (page 116)
Mephitis mephitis — striped skunk (page 118)
Mustela erminea — common weasel, ermine or stoat (page 111)
Mustela putorius — European polecat (page 113)
Mustela vison — eastern mink (page 112)
Spilogale putorius — spotted skunk (page 119)
Taxidae taxus — American badger (page 117)
Tayra barbara — tayra (page 115)

VIVERRIDAE: civets, genets and mongooses (35-37 genera, 74-82 species)
Civettictis civetta — African civet (page 122)
Herpestes ichneumon — African mongoose (page 123)

HYAENIDAE: hyenas and aardwolf (3 genera, 4 species)
(including the aardwolf (1 genus, 1 species) , sometimes separated
as family PROTELIDAE)
Crocuta crocuta — spotted or laughing hyena (page 124)
Hyaena hyaena — striped hyena (page 125)

FELIDAE: cats and relatives (2-6 genera, 35-40 species)
Acinonyx jubatus — cheetah or hunting leopard (page 141)
Felis concolor — puma or mountain lion (page 132)
Felis margarita — sand cat (page 127)
Felis pardalis — ocelot (page 130)
Felis serval — serval (page 128)
Felis viverrina — fishing cat (page 129)
Felis yagouaroundi — jaguarundi (page 131)

Lynx canadensis — Canada lynx (page 126)
Neofelis nebulosa — clouded leopard (page 139)
Panthera leo — lion (page 138)
Panthera onca — jaguar (page 133)
Panthera pardus — leopard (page 134)
Panthera tigris tigris — tiger (pages 136-137)
Panthera tigris longipilis — Siberian tiger (page 135)
Uncia uncia — snow leopard or ounce (page 140)

order **PINNIPEDIA:** aquatic flesh-eating mammals or pinnipeds (3 families, 17-21 genera, 31-33 species)
(sometimes included in order CARNIVORA as a suborder)

families: OTARIIDAE: eared or fur seals and sea lions (6-7 genera, 12-14 species)
Callorhinus ursinus — northern fur seal (page 143)
Zalophus californianus — California sea lion (page 142)

ODOBENIDAE: walrus (1 genus, 1 species)
Odobenus rosmarus — walrus (page 144)

PHOCIDAE: true, earless or hair seals (10-13 genera, 18 species)
Mirounga angustirostris — northern sea elephant (page 146)
Phoca vitulina — harbor seal (page 145)

order **CONDYLARTHRA**

order **LITOPTERNA**

order **NOTOUNGULATA**

order **ASTRAPOTHERIA**

order **TUBULIDENTATA:** aardvark (1 family, 1 genus, 1 species)

family: ORYCTEROPODIDAE (or ORYCTEROPIDAE) : aardvark (1 genus, 1 species)
Orycteropus afer — aardvark (page 147)

order **PANTODONTA (or AMBLYPODA)**

order **DINOCERATA**

order **PYROTHERIA**

order **PROBOSCIDEA:** elephants (1 family, 2 genera, 2 species)

family: ELEPHANTIDAE: elephants (2 genera, 2 species)
Elephas maximus — Indian or Asiatic elephant (page 149)
Loxodonta africana — African elephant (page 150)

order **EMBRITHOPODA**

order **HYRACOIDEA:** hyraxes (1 family, 3 genera, 9-12 species)

family: PROCAVIIDAE (or HYRACIDAE) : hyraxes (3 genera, 9-12 species)
Heterohyrax brucei — rock hyrax (page 151)

order **SIRENIA:** sea cows (2 families, 2 genera, 4 species)

families: DUGONGIDAE: dugong (1 genus, 1 species)
(reports of the continued existence of a second genus and species,
Steller's sea cow (Hydrodamalis gigas or stelleri) are unconfirmed)
Dugong dugon — dugong (page 152)

TRICHECHIDAE: manatees (1 genus, 3 species)
Trichechus manatus — North American or Florida manatee (page 153)

order **PERISSODACTYLA:** odd-toed hoofed mammals or ungulates (3 families, 6 genera, 16-18 species)

families: EQUIDAE: horses and relatives (1 genus, 7-8 species)
Equus burchelli — Grant's zebra (page 156)
Equus hemionus kiang — kiang (page 158)
Equus hemionus onager — onager (page 157)
Equus przewalskii — Asiatic wild horse (page 155)

TAPIRIDAE: tapirs (1 genus, 4-5 species)
Tapirus indicus — Malayan tapir (page 160)
Tapirus terrestris — Brazilian tapir (page 159)

RHINOCEROTIDAE: rhinoceroses (4 genera, 5 species)
Diceros bicornis — African black rhinoceros (page 162)
Rhinoceros unicornis — Indian or one-horned rhinoceros (page 161)

order **ARTIODACTYLA:** even-toed hoofed mammals or ungulates (9 families, 75-82 genera, 171-210 species)

families: SUIDAE: pigs and hogs (5 genera, 8-9 species)
Phacochoerus aethiopicus — wart hog (page 164)
Sus scrofa — wild boar (page 163)

TAYASSUIDAE: peccaries (1 genus, 2 species)
Tayassu tajacu — collared peccary (page 165)

HIPPOPOTAMIDAE: hippopotami (2 genera, 2 species)
Hippopotamus amphibius — hippopotamus (page 166)

CAMELIDAE: camels and llamas (2-3 genera, 4-6 species)
Camelus bactrianus — Bactrian or two-humped camel (page 168)
Camelus dromedarius — dromedary or one-humped camel (page 167)
Lama guanacoe — guanaco (page 169)
Lama pacos — alpaca (page 171)
Lama peruana — llama (page 170)
Vicugna vicugna — vicuña (page 172)

TRAGULIDAE: mouse deer or chevrotains (2 genera, 4-7 species)

CERVIDAE: deer and relatives (16-17 genera, 37-53 species)
Alces alces — moose (page 176)
Cervus elaphus — European red deer (page 173)
Odocoileus hemionus — mule deer (page 175)
Odocoileus virginianus — American white-tailed or Virginia deer (page 174)
Rangifer tarandus — caribou or reindeer (page 177)

GIRAFFIDAE: giraffe and okapi (2 genera, 2 species)
Giraffa camelopardalis — giraffe (page 179)
Okapia johnstoni — okapi (page 178)

ANTILOCAPRIDAE: pronghorn or American antelope (1 genus, 1 species)
Antilocapra americana — pronghorn antelope (page 180)

BOVIDAE: true or Old World antelopes, cattle, sheep, goats and buffaloes
(44-49 genera, 111-128 species)
Aepyceros melampus — impala (page 198)
Alcelaphus buselaphus — red hartebeest (page 193)
Ammotragus lervia — Barbary sheep or aoudad (page 206)
Antidorcas marsupialis — springbuck or springbok (page 200)
Antilope cervicapra — blackbuck or Indian antelope (page 197)
Bison bison — American bison (page 190)
Bison bonasus — European bison or wisent (page 191)
Bos banteng — banteng (page 188)
Bos gaurus — gaur (page 187)

Bos grunniens — yak (page 186)
Bos indicus — zebu or Brahma cattle (page 185)
Boselaphus tragocamelus — nilgai or bluebuck (page 183)
Bubalus bubalis — water buffalo (page 184)
Capra (or Orthaegoceros) falconeri — markhor (page 205)
Capra ibex — ibex (page 204)
Connochaetes taurinus — white-bearded gnu or wildebeest (page 194)
Litocranius walleri — gerenuk or Waller's gazelle (page 199)
Neotragus batesi — Bates' pygmy antelope (page 196)
Oreamnos americanus — Rocky Mountain goat (page 201)
Oreotragus oreotragus — klipspringer (page 195)
Oryx gazella — gemsbok (page 192)
Ovibos moschatus — musk ox (page 203)
Ovis canadensis — bighorn sheep (page 207)
Ovis musimon — mouflon (page 208)
Rupicapra rupicapra — chamois (page 202)
Syncerus caffer — African buffalo (page 189)
Taurotragus oryx — common eland (page 182)
Tragelaphus strepsiceros — greater kudu (page 181)

Index

This book was published by Hammond Incorporated under the following editorial direction: Ashley F. Talbot, *Executive Editor;* Charles G. Lees, *Managing Editor;* H. George Stoll, *Map Editor;* Isabelle Reid, *Book Designer;* Emily D. Highfield, *Copy Editor.*

All creative operations were coordinated by Andrew F. Kuber in cooperation with Herbert Pierce, *Director of Carto Arts,* and Edmund Ballman, *Director of Photography. Graphics* by Nicholas Zarrelli, Elizabeth Streeter and Stanley Ziemolozynski. *Color Separation* by Dieter Hoefer. *Photography* by Lou Zavis, William Theofilas and Daniel Bauer. Type was set in Mergenthaler's 11 pt. Scotch No. 2 in the composing room of Hammond Press.

The paper was made specially for the book by Weyerhaeuser Company, Tacoma, Washington. It was printed by Zabel Bros., and bound by Van Rees Book Binding Corporation.